(front cover) The nuclear submarine
HMS *Repulse*. Photo: HMS *Neptune*/
MoD

(back cover) HMS *Ark Royal* (rear)
passes *Eagle* on leaving Devonport for
the major NATO exercise 'Teamwork
70'. Photo: HMS *Ark Royal*

(front and back endpapers) HMS *Ark
Royal* at the beginning of her career
(1955) and at the end (1978). Enormous
changes took place in the intervening
years: suppression of the port deck-
edge lift, progressive removal of her
4.5-inch and 40-mm guns, and replacement of nearly all her radar. Some
changes were dictated by operational
needs, others by the need for more
internal space.
(Drawn by John A. Roberts)

ISBN 0 11 290319 3

Design by HMSO Graphic Design

Printed in England for
Her Majesty's Stationery Office
by W. S. Cowell Ltd, Ipswich

Dd 596286   K160

AD FINEM FIDELIS

Hurl

National Maritime Museum

THE SHIP

Dreadnought to Nuclear Submarine

Antony Preston

London
Her Majesty's Stationery Office

Contents

(right) The battleship HMS *Resolution* in 1921. Photo: NMM/R.Perkins

Introduction by the General Editor

This is the ninth of a series of ten short books on the development of the ship, both the merchant vessel and the specialized vessel of war, from the earliest times to the present day, commissioned and produced jointly by the National Maritime Museum and Her Majesty's Stationery Office.

The books are each self-contained, each dealing with one aspect of the subject, but together they cover the evolution of vessels in terms which are detailed, accurate and up-to-date. They incorporate the latest available information and the latest thinking on the subject, but they are readily intelligible to the non-specialist, professional historian or layman.

Above all, as should be expected from the only large and comprehensive general historical museum in the world which deals essentially with the impact of the sea on the development of human culture and civilization, the approach is unromantic and realistic. Merchant ships were and are machines for carrying cargo profitably. They carried the trade and, in the words of the very distinguished author of the second book in this series, 'the creation of wealth through trade is at the root of political and military power'. The vessel of war, the maritime vehicle of that power, follows and she is a machine for men to fight from, or with.

It follows from such an approach that the illustrations to the series are for the most part from contemporary sources. The reader can form his own conclusions from the evidence, written and visual. We have not commissioned hypothetical reconstructions, the annotation of which, done properly, would take up quite a percentage of the text.

In this ninth book of the series, Antony Preston deals with the development of warships in the 20th century. Once again the centre of the scene is in Britain, but, as with all the authors in the series, the approach is broadly international. Shipping and shipbuilding are international businesses in which developments in one country spread rapidly all over the world. Most especially has this been true of warships in the 20th century, when nations have used great resources to endeavour to determine what developments were taking place in the navies of their potential rivals, though, as the book clearly shows, governments have not always been quick to benefit from the information they have gained from either covert or overt sources or from battle experience. The author gives a lucid account of international rivalry and of technical development frequently impeded in its application by political considerations. This book is particularly well illustrated and the author's authoritative captions add valuable detail to the general account given in the text.

Antony Preston, formerly on the Staff of the National Maritime Museum and now a freelance historian, is one of the established authorities on this particular part of maritime history, about which he writes with such clarity and thoroughness.

Basil Greenhill
DIRECTOR, NATIONAL MARITIME MUSEUM
General Editor

Once the keel of the *Dreadnought* was laid on 2 October 1905 work proceeded rapidly. Soon, the frames of the double bottom were laid on the building slip and the first bulkheads could be erected. Photo: NMM

Before the end of the first month the frames for the armoured deck were in position, with the supporting plating riveted in place. Photo: NMM

Looking forward along the upper deck the forecastle can be seen, with openings in the deck for boiler uptakes and gun turrets. It is now 29 January 1906. Photo: NMM

The ship was launched on 10th February 1906 and immediately she was transferred to a fitting-out dock for the installation of machinery and armament, as well as the myriad items of equipment. The stern view is dated 9 April. Photo: NMM

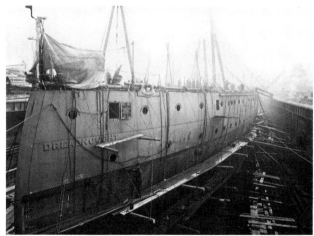

Age of the Dreadnought

On 30 December 1905 the distinctive ram bow is complete and part of the forecastle. The *Dreadnought* has been under construction for less than three months. Photo: NMM

Finally, the gaunt but impressive profile of HMS *Dreadnought* takes shape, with twin 12-inch gun turrets aboard and power available to train them. Note also the shelf and booms for anti-torpedo nets. The date 11 August 1906, four months before completion. Photo: NMM

The British battleship *Dreadnought* gave her name to a whole era of warships, and both she and her most ardent advocate, Lord Fisher, rightly deserve their place in history. But HMS *Dreadnought* was nothing more than the culmination of a series of trends in ship-technology, and the decade 1904 to 1914 also saw changes to all other types of warship.

At the turn of the century the trend in large warships had been towards bigger and better-armed cruisers, and to meet the threat from their medium-calibre guns the battleships of all navies had begun to strengthen the 'secondary' armament, while at the same time retaining the guns of 5- to 6-inch calibre as a 'tertiary' battery for defence against torpedo-boats and destroyers. But these three levels of armament produced their own problems. In the 1890s advances in the chemical industry had at last produced slow-burning cordite propellant for guns, and because it burned at a more precise rate it was much easier to predict the fall of shot at long range. As late as 1903 battleships still practised their main gunnery at a range of 3 to 4000 yards – not as so often thought, because it was the Trafalgar range, but because accurate shooting was impossible at greater ranges with the old fast-burning powders.

By 1904 the gunnery experts in the Royal Navy and the United States Navy were well aware of the opportunities opening up, but the only way of aiming guns at extreme ranges (up to ten miles) was to spot the shell-splashes and correct accordingly. The secondary guns (typically 8- to 10-inch calibre) produced shell-splashes which were almost indistinguishable from those made by the main armament (normally 12- to 13.5-inch calibre). Most modern battleships at the turn of the century mounted two twin heavy guns, and it became obvious that a uniform armament of major guns, without the intermediate calibres, would make long-range gunfire much easier.

There was a third factor, which in the long run was to have the most lasting influence, a major improvement in propulsion. The big reciprocating steam engine was nearing the limit of development, but naval tactics still called for higher and higher speeds. A British engineer, the Hon. Charles Parsons, had revived an ancient idea, the steam turbine, and as the movement of this type of machinery was purely rotary it suffered much less from the vibration which plagued all high-speed ships at the end of the 19th century.

The Royal Navy was quick to grasp the potential of the Parsons turbine, and between 1899 and 1904 completed four destroyers and a light cruiser with the new machinery. As a result, when the First Sea Lord, Admiral Fisher, decided that the *Dreadnought's* speed was to be 21 knots instead of the usual 18 knots, the machinery-designers had sufficient confidence to accept the challenge. The risk was immense, for no merchant ship of comparable tonnage had yet been engined with the Parsons turbine. The Royal Navy's competitors did not share its boldness, and the Germans, Americans and French clung to the triple-expansion engine for much longer.

The turbine made another giant stride possible. The armoured cruiser was a dangerous foe to all but the most powerful battleships, and to Admiral Fisher it seemed logical to build a new type of ship which was faster than existing cruisers and better-armed. The result was the 'dreadnought armoured cruiser', for already the *Dreadnought* had given her name to a new generation of ships. HMS *Invincible*, the

prototype, was a turbine-driven development from the previous class of armoured cruisers, rather than an evolution from the *Dreadnought* herself, but in his enthusiasm for gun power Fisher insisted that she should have the same 12-inch guns.

The clumsy name eventually gave way to the term 'battlecruiser' in 1913 but this gave a totally artificial impression that these handsome ships, with their heavy armament and cruiser-scale armour, were a type of fast battleship. Although Fisher was vague about how to employ the battlecruisers, it was felt that their 12-inch guns would enable them to sweep aside cruisers when scouting for the main fleet, to gain a tactical advantage or to finish off damaged battleships. What happened in practice was that the battlecruisers came to be thought of as 'capital ships', and their weaknesses were conveniently overlooked. The German Navy, being the chief rival of the Royal Navy, immediately copied the idea, but remedied their basic weakness by striking a better balance between speed and armour.

The impact of the *Dreadnought* and the battlecruiser on other warships was profound. Between 1903 and 1908 the speed of the battle fleet had jumped from 18 knots to 21 knots, and so the margin of speed for scouting cruisers and destroyers had to keep pace. The British and Germans began to build a series of light cruisers, all named after towns; they were capable of 24–25 knots, and were armed with medium-calibre guns, although the British preferred a heavier armament than the Germans. The British destroyer, having eliminated the frailties of the early type in the robust $25\frac{1}{2}$ knot 'River' Class of 1903, was now regarded as too slow, and speed was increased to 27 knots. The only retrograde step was at the instigation of Fisher, when in an excess of enthusiasm for oil fuel he ordered a batch of 33-knotters, the first 'Tribal' Class. To achieve such a jump in speed they had to sacrifice armament, seaworthiness and endurance, with the result that when war came in 1914 they could only be used in the English Channel.

Armour also had an important part to play in the evolution of this new generation of warships, although after 1908 there were few major advances in the field of metallurgy to affect the quality of the armour itself. The problems stemmed from the advances made in weapons, for in addition to the 'race' between armour and armour-piercing shells there was the growing power of the torpedo.

To take the gun first, the trend at the end of the previous century had been to reduce the calibre of big guns from the very large (13-inch to 17.7-inch) down to 12-inch, but with longer barrels to impart a

The German dreadnought battleship *Oldenburg*, although laid down over three years after the *Dreadnought*, was still driven by triple-expansion engines and could only bring the same broadside to bear. However, she and her sisters had 11 feet more beam, which permitted better underwater protection. Photo: Drüppel

higher velocity to the shell and to take advantage of the improved propellants already mentioned. Thus the *Dreadnought's* main armament of ten 12-inch guns was similar in character to her immediate predecessors, and her only superiority lay in having more of them, which in turn enabled her to fight at a longer range. Gun-designers were constantly experimenting with longer barrels, new shells and different methods of making guns, but as a twin turret and all its training, elevating and loading machinery weighed over 500 tons and took two to three years to construct, improvements were carefully considered.

The torpedo, which was the original Whitehead 'fish' torpedo of the 1870s, had been developing even more rapidly than the gun. From being an erratic weapon with a practical range of only 800 yards it became more accurate, and by 1908 the British 21-inch Mk I could reach 3500 yards at a speed of 45 knots. The main cause for this startling improvement was the 'heater' system, introduced in the United States and Great Britain at roughly the same time (about 1904). The same compressed-air drive was used, but by burning fuel in the compressed air before it entered the combustion pot much greater power was produced. In step with this improved performance greater directional accuracy was obtained as the quality of gyroscopes improved. The much greater range of the torpedo went almost unnoticed, but it was to have a profound effect on naval tactics, for hitherto it had been confined to use at night or in poor visibility, since daylight attack would be suicidal against light rapid-firing guns. Now a destroyer might be able to fire her torpedoes at maximum range and turn away before the target's secondary batteries could register a hit.

When the *Dreadnought* was designed it was felt that the flimsy destroyers of the day did not merit anything but the lightest defensive armament of 3-inch guns, and this was the view of the designers

7

of her near contemporaries, the USS *Michigan* and *South Carolina*. The phrase 'all-big gun' ships was taken literally, and there was to be no intermediate calibre. But, as so often happens, theory was outstripped by practice, and when destroyers grew larger and more robust it was realised that a puny 3-inch shell lacked hitting power. Within a year or two the medium-calibre secondary gun was making its appearance once more. The Germans were the only ones who remained faithful to the medium-calibre gun throughout, and all their dreadnoughts and battlecruisers had a heavy armament of 5.9-inch guns.

In the midst of all this feverish technological progress Russia became involved in a war with Japan, and for the first time since 1866 major warships of modern design fought one another. There

The British battlecruiser *Inflexible* (seen here at Sheerness alongside the light cruiser *Chester*) was regarded as almost equal to the *Dreadnought* on account of her 12-inch guns and 25 knots' speed. But the original specification was merely for a turbine-driven armoured cruiser with heavy guns, and so the *Invincible* Class proved incapable of facing battleships. Photo: Imperial War Museum

was plenty of action of various kinds to test theories of ship-design, from mine-damage to magazines exploded by direct hits from land-based howitzers, but undoubtedly the most influential event was the Battle of Tsushima in May 1905. As with the previous naval battle, Lissa in 1866, nearly all the conclusions drawn were incorrect or misleading.

The point which struck every observer was the fact that the Japanese Fleet had opened fire on the Russians at 7000 yards, justifying all the predictions of gunnery experts. Other points were glossed over, such as the fact that Japanese armour-piercing shells had fuzes that were too sensitive to guarantee penetration of thick armour. Above all, opinion in America and Great Britain was on the side of the 'gallant little Japanese' in their fight against mighty Russia. The Russian Baltic Fleet was in a parlous state before the battle, and it was forced to allow the Japanese to manoeuvre at will, whereas a more resolute opponent could have taken advantage of several Japanese mistakes. But the most important lesson of all went unheeded. Examination of both Japanese and Russian ships showed that damage below the waterline caused progressive flooding, and as many compartments were only theoretically watertight, it was possible for a ship to sink much faster than expected.

The reason for the oversight was partly complacency and partly the pace of technical advance. After all, the West had taught Japan all she knew, and in any case the ships which fought at Tsushima were quite outclassed by the new *Dreadnought* under construction. The detailed reports on repairs to the Tsushima casualties sent to the Royal Navy in 1905 were not translated from the Japanese until 1917, by which time the Battle of Jutland had re-demonstrated many of the salient points.

The obvious proof that battleships could engage at ranges of 7000 yards or more spurred the gun-designers on to greater efforts. One school of thought still favoured a greater number of guns, and using higher velocities to carry the shell further. Thus the first German replies to the *Dreadnought* carried twelve 11-inch guns, as against her ten 12-inch. The British tried to improve their 12-inch gun by lengthening it, but this proved a retrograde step as the gun suffered from 'whip' and could not be relied on for accurate long-range shooting. To cure this it was decided to go to a bigger and heavier shell, and the result was the re-introduction of the 13.5-inch gun, last used nearly twenty years before. Even in its initial form, with a relatively light shell, it proved to be much more accurate than the 12-inch and had the additional advantage of greater destructive power. Other navies took the hint, and the US and Japanese navies adopted a 14-inch gun of very similar characteristics. The Germans, however, clung to their ideas about high velocities and light shells, and only moved up to 12-inch calibre.

As the gun alone weighed nearly 10 tons more than the old 12-inch, and the turrets were in similar proportion, the change of calibre implied a big increase in size, if the same number of guns and the same basic qualities of speed and armour were not to be reduced. Every navy is administered by a government which grudges the money spent on new ships, and inevitably the ship-designers were told to find ways of restricting the growth of battleships. The *Dreadnought* had been typical of her generation in having two of her five gun-mountings on the beam to enable them to fire ahead, astern and on the beam, whereas the contemporary USS *Michigan* achieved nearly the same concentration of gunpower by having only four twin turrets. The difference was that in the *Michigan* all four turrets were on the centreline, with No. 2 and No. 3 raised by one deck level, or 'superfiring'. This meant that all eight guns could fire on either broadside, without the strain and blast-damage to the hull from firing the wing guns.

Bigger guns meant not only greater ranges but greater penetration of armour, and so attention had to be paid to armouring the sides and decks. There were those, such as Fisher and the advocates of the battlecruiser, who claimed that 'speed is armour', and that a fast ship could choose the range at which she would fight. But as long as the big gun was the most powerful weapon afloat the battle fleet would continue to form the main strategic weapon, and to function most effectively it had to concentrate its gunpower. To do this meant manoeuvring in close order, with all the discipline and centralized control possible. According to Fisher only two warship-types

By 1911 gun calibres had risen from 12-inch to 13.5-inch and then 14-inch, a trend which forced both the British and the Germans to plan for a further jump to 15-inch guns in 1912. The Chilean battleship *Almirante Latorre* was 10 000 tons heavier than the *Dreadnought*, and ships of similar power were building for many navies. As HMS *Canada* the ship served in the Royal Navy until 1918 and subsequently returned to Chilean ownership; when scrapped in 1959 she was the last major Jutland veteran. Photo: NMM

were needed, the battlecruiser and the super-destroyer, but fortunately for all concerned this extreme doctrine was never put into effect, and the full range of types continued to be built.

The battlecruiser kept pace with the battleship throughout this period and adopted the bigger guns as they became available. When the *Lion* class were built in 1909-12 they were some 4000 tons bigger and over 100 feet longer than their battleship equivalents, the *Orion* Class. These anomalies led to the introduction of the term 'battleship cruiser', and finally battlecruiser, while the popular press termed them and the *Orions* 'super-dreadnoughts'.

Not content with the 13.5-inch gun, the Royal Navy decided in 1911 to achieve a decisive margin over its rivals by arming the next class of battleships with a 15-inch gun. But this meant guns weighing nearly 100 tons each and 750-ton turrets, and it was obvious that displacement was in danger of rising too sharply. Not only was cost crucial, but such mundane matters as docking, for ships were growing too big to get into many existing docks. As docks were an unglamorous part of naval expenditure money for alterations to them was hard to find. The docking of big ships for periodic repairs presented the major navies with a constant headache, and the growth of size in battleships even forced the German Government to spend ten years on widening the Kiel Canal in order to preserve the freedom to move squadrons in and out of the Baltic with ease.

As so often happens, one step forward facilitates a second, and when the British came to consider building a 15-inch gunned battleship it was pointed out that it would be possible to drop one twin gun turret and still have a broadside of 15 000 lbs of shells, more than ten of the latest 13.5-inch guns. The question then arose of what to do with the space left amidships, and the engineers pointed out that it could be filled with more boilers to produce higher

speed than the standard 21 knots. In turn the War College advised that a speed of 25 knots would enable a battleship squadron to act as a proper 'fast wing' of the battle fleet, to work ahead of the main body or to catch up. These would be true fast battleships, not thinly plated battlecruisers, and the decision was made to build no more of these impressive but vulnerable and costly hybrids.

Making the decision was not easy, for 25 knots was asking a lot of the steam turbines of the day, only eight years after the first large units had been designed. The problems could be considerably eased by changing from coal to oil fuel; with its higher thermal efficiency oil would make high speed easier to attain, and as it weighed less than coal the difference could be devoted to thicker armour. Unknown to the British, this argument also swayed the American designers of a new super-dreadnought, the USS *Nevada*, which could only be built on the tonnage fixed by Congress if 1700 tons' weight was saved. Oil had been used for some years, first in Russian battleships, and latterly in British ships, but it was sprayed on the coal fires to boost top speed and had never been the main fuel.

(right) The introduction of the diesel engine in the French submarine *Aigrette* in 1904 marked a big improvement in safety. It provided a light propulsion unit for surface-running and charging the batteries, but without the dangerous vapour from petrol engines. Photo: Marius Bar

Submarines come of age

One class of warship has been left out of the story so far. The submarine had been little more than a toy at the turn of the century, and despite interesting results on manoeuvres the limitations of size alone meant that these small craft were fit only for harbour defence. Admiral Fisher himself had used the existence of submarines as a pretext for abolishing the mine-defences of Great Britain, with the result that for some years the Royal Navy paid no attention to developments in mines and built a considerable number of small coastal submarines.

The French had been the first to develop submarines at the end of the 1880's, followed closely by the Americans, who had more success. The British plumped for the American designs, which had the disadvantage of using a gasoline engine for running on the surface. In the confined space of a submarine the inflammable vapour was highly dangerous, and it was not until the German Rudolf Diesel perfected a compression-ignition motor which used less volatile or 'heavy' oil that a safe lightweight propulsion system was available. Despite being a German invention the Diesel engine was first adopted by the French for the submarine *Aigrette* in 1904; not until 1912, after the Russians, British and Americans had taken it up, did the Germans finally change over.

The Germans came into the submarine game quite late, but profited by other people's mistakes. Even so, their early U-boats were no better suited to work outside coastal waters. The British found that the simplest solution was to increase the size of the submarine; by reducing the strain on the crew there was a noticeable increase in efficiency, and more space could be devoted to fuel and stores.

Even so, the submarine was a primitive fighting ship compared to surface ships. A newsreel film taken in Germany in 1917 shows a mechanic coming on deck covered literally from head to foot in grease, and

Despite their pioneering work the French found the diesel engine unreliable and soon reverted to steam for surface propulsion. The *Espadon*'s small conning tower almost obscures the collapsible funnel which was covered by a watertight hatch before diving. French submarines were also the last to be fitted with internal tubes for launching torpedoes, and the Drzewiecki 'drop-collars' can be seen on either side of the deck-casing. Photo: Imperial War Museum

photographs taken at sea give some indication of the squalor and misery of an extended-cruise. Condensation made bedding wet and turned food mouldy, and yet submariners took a fierce pride in their discomfort. When in harbour the worst conditions could be mitigated by providing such basic necessities as baths, showers and one bunk per man (as opposed to the 'hot bunk' system of two men taking turns between watches) on board a submarine tender.

As early as 1900 the French had tried to increase the submarine's endurance by providing a lightweight steam engine for surface running. This boat, the *Narval*, took about 20 minutes to prepare for diving, but in later boats compressed air cooling was provided to cut the time down to less than 10 minutes. Several of these steam-driven submarines were built before 1914 but only by the French. In 1912–13 the British made a comprehensive review of their policy about submarine designs and decided that there was no place for the small coastal submarine. Instead they wanted a medium-sized boat of 500–600 tons with a surface speed of 14–15 knots capable of offensive operations in the North Sea.

One obvious use for submarines was in conjunction with surface ships, accompanying them on the surface and diving when the enemy fleet approached, to allow them to pick off damaged ships and stragglers. But this was not possible with diesel-engined submarines as they lacked the power for more than 14–15 knots. In 1913 Vickers produced a design for a submarine driven by steam turbines, capable of 23 knots; it was like the French boats but used a more advanced boiler which could be shut down immediately, and so could dive almost as fast as a diesel-engined boat. The idea was shelved for the moment but not forgotten.

The Admiralty took the unusual step of taking out licences from Italian and French designers to stimulate development, and the idea was copied by other navies. For example, the Americans bought an Italian boat, the Italians bought a German boat and the Danes bought an American design built in Austria. This exchange of information reflected the fact that the submarine used the most advanced naval technology; good design relied much more on the quality of the components like engines and periscopes than on the traditional skills of the shipbuilder.

Despite the interest shown by all navies in submarines little thought was given to how to use them, apart from the largely theoretical idea of ambushing a hostile fleet or defending the approaches to a harbour. The Royal Navy provided one of its submarines with a light gun as early as 1912 and the Germans fitted some of their early U-boats with a small gun on a folding mounting which disappeared into the deck-casing when the boat dived. The idea was that submarines could help to enforce a blockade, and to do this it would be helpful to fire the traditional 'shot across the bows' of a merchantman. There was, however, no suggestion that submarines could be used to sink merchant shipping indiscriminately, and the main target of all submarines was assumed to be warships.

Submarine-building was an international business. These Canadian submarines, *CH.14* and *CH.15* were built in Montreal to an American Bethlehem design, which was also built for the US Navy, the Chileans and Italians as well as the Royal Navy. Photo: Canadian Forces

The light cruiser HMS *Royalist*, one of the new *Arethusa* Class which started a new line of development in 1912. Although cramped and lively in a seaway, they bore the brunt of North Sea operations and proved capable of taking heavy punishment. Photo: MoD

Experience of war

Everyone expected a clash of the British and German fleets within hours of the outbreak of war, and when this did not occur there was a noticeable sense of anti-climax on both sides. For one thing, the Royal Navy removed its main fleet to a new base in the Orkneys, where it was less exposed to attrition from submarine and surface torpedo-attacks but also well placed to block any move by German forces into the Atlantic. The southern half of the North Sea was not abandoned but it could safely be left to cruisers, destroyers and submarines.

As hopes of an early victory faded both sides took stock. The Germans stepped up their minelaying efforts and ordered more U-boats, for their aim was to whittle down the numerical superiority of the British battle fleet to a point where it could be engaged by their own High Seas Fleet with safety. The British for their part had to safeguard their lines of supply from the Empire and across to France, for the bulk of their army was fighting alongside the French.

The German Army's right flank on the Belgian coast was vulnerable to naval bombardment, and soon a motley collection of old gunboats were sent over from England to shell targets that presented themselves. From this came the idea of building special bombarding ships armed with the heaviest guns. As they resembled the old *Monitor* of the American Civil War they were christened monitors, a type which had been defunct in the Royal Navy for over 30 years. The supply of guns could have been a problem, but out of the blue came an offer from the American Bethlehem Steel Company to sell four twin 14-inch guns ordered by Greece for a battleship building in Germany. The chance was seized, and all four mountings arrived in England before the end of 1914 labelled as agricultural machinery. There was a surplus of elderly battleships, whose crews were needed for newer ships, and four of these were stripped of their 12-inch guns to arm another eight monitors.

The Germans also found that their old battleships were a liability because of their demands on manpower, and so they were progressively decommissioned and disarmed. The guns were always useful for coast defence and long-range bombardment, and as the German Navy was short of base-facilities many of these old ships became accommodation hulks.

The battlecruiser seemed to be the best type of offensive ship, for at the Battle of the Falklands the *Invincible* and *Inflexible* destroyed the German armoured cruisers *Scharnhorst* and *Gneisenau* after they in turn had sunk two old British cruisers at Coronel the month before. Then in January 1915 the rival battlecruisers clashed in the Battle of the Dogger Bank, resulting in the sinking of the armoured cruiser *Blücher*. What was not obvious was that in both actions the victims had been obsolescent cruisers, the proper prey of these 'dreadnought armoured cruisers'. The emphasis on long-range shooting also meant a great deal of ammunition expended for a very low percentage of hits, and on both occasions decisive hits had only been obtained when the range came down.

The British had cause to be thankful that they had reversed Fisher's policy of not building cruisers after

1908. A series of well-designed light cruisers had replaced the obsolescent armoured cruiser, armed with 6-inch guns and torpedoes and capable of 25 knots. The Germans had followed suit with ships of similar size and performance but because of the theoretical advantage of a 'hail of fire' had clung to the 10.5-cm (4.1-inch) gun. The folly of this was shown in November 1914 when the Australian cruiser *Sydney* easily outranged the German *Emden* at Cocos-Keeling Island and destroyed her. In the many skirmishes which took place in the North Sea the British light cruisers could also outrange their opponents, and although belated efforts were made to re-equip some ships with 15-cm (5.9-inch) guns the balance was never redressed.

The British cruisers had shown a steady improvement in each design since 1908. The original ships had been protected against shellfire by a steel deck over the boilers and turbines, and by 1910 it was possible to provide a narrow strip of 3-inch armour along the waterline as well. The purpose was to protect the machinery against light shells, rather than to enable the ship to survive a heavy pounding, for a cruiser's most valuable asset was her speed. In 1912 there was a revision of policy, and it was decided that 30-knot cruisers were needed to work with battle-cruisers and the new fast destroyers.

The figure of 30 knots was over-optimistic, but the effort to reach it resulted in a significant improvement in design. By using destroyer-type turbines and boilers it was possible to boost horsepower from 25 000 to 40 000, in a hull which was 20 feet shorter and 10 feet narrower than the current *Chatham* class. By working the armour longitudinally as part of the structure instead of bolting the armour to the plating, it was possible to have a greater area of 3-inch armour than before. The new ships were such an improvement that they were known for a while as 'light armoured cruisers', and as the *Arethusa* class they proved ideal for the North Sea. The inevitable sacrifice had to be made for such a leap forward, and the *Arethusa* had only two 6-inch guns and six 4-inch. She was wet in rough weather and because of the restriction on size to 3500 tons was cramped and uncomfortable.

In fact both the 25-knot 'Towns' and the 29-knot *Arethusas* served with the main fleet in the North Sea and gave good service. The *Arethusa* proved an ideal

HMS *Lowestoft* was one of the last of the four-funnelled 'Town' type of cruiser built from 1908. Although not provided for in Fisher's plans for the Royal Navy they proved to have a very important rôle in the First World War as fleet escorts and scouts. Because they were bigger and more seaworthy they outlasted the *Arethusa* Class by more than a decade, despite being older ships. Photo: NMM

basis for expansion, and the design was improved through no fewer than seven subsequent classes, a total of 44 ships. Very little was done beyond adding a little more beam each time for stability and lengthening the hull to make space for more armament, but at the end of the process the two 6-inch guns had become six and tonnage had grown from 3500 to 4650, all on the same horsepower and speed.

The Germans contented themselves with developing their *Frankfurt* class, 5200-tonners with eight 15-cm guns. But the pace of building was slow, and by 1918 only 11 had been completed. The only other cruisers built were the two fast minelayers *Brummer* and *Bremse*. They were not part of the pre-war programme, but were suggested as a means of using four sets of turbines building for the Russian battle-cruiser *Navarin*: with two sets of turbines each they developed 47000 h.p. and reached 28 knots on 4400 tons. A resemblance to the British *Arethusa* class was deliberately fostered, even to the extent of having a folding mainmast.

The U-boat quickly established itself as a much more potent weapon than anyone had imagined. The first days were a disappointment, and an attempt to take 10 U-boats as far as the Shetlands was a failure. One boat was sent home with faulty engines, one was rammed by a British cruiser and one was sunk, probably by a mine. Another patrol two days later, intended to catch British troopships taking the BEF across to France was equally fruitless, with only one out of four boats able to reach her patrol area without breaking down.

However frustrating these early patrols were they tested equipment and showed up faults, and by their very lack of success lulled the Royal Navy into a false sense of security. This was dispelled abruptly when on 22 September, 1914, a solitary U-boat, *U.9*, sank three big armoured cruisers, the *Aboukir*, *Cressy* and *Hogue*. Within a quarter of an hour this 500-ton boat sank three 12000-ton ships and drowned 1300 men.

It was not the end for the surface warship, but it did mark the end of the days in which an enemy could be seen before an action started, and it showed that ships could no longer use the seas freely. The immediate solution was to order all ships to zig-zag and make alterations of speed and course whenever the presence of a submarine was suspected.

The Japanese not only sent destroyers to the Mediterranean to help the Allies against the Austro-Hungarian Fleet but even built destroyers for the French. These *Kaba* Class at Corfu in 1917 had their counterparts in the French *Arabe* Class. Photo: Imperial War Museum

Destroyers were found to be very difficult targets for U-boats on account of their manoeuvrability and shallow draught, and although their only suitable weapons were the gun and the ram they scored the first successes against U-boats. It became standard procedure for the Grand Fleet to proceed with a large screen of destroyers, and this was so successful that throughout the War the whole Grand Fleet lost only two cruisers to U-boat attack while at sea with its destroyer screen.

The next step was to find a way of limiting the damage done by a torpedo-hit. The 'bulge' had first been tried in 1913, a light casing attached to the ship's side below the waterline, filled with air and water compartments. The outer air-filled space absorbed the explosion some distance from the main hull, while the inner water-filled space absorbed any splinters and distributed the force of the explosion over a larger area. Bulges were first fitted to the monitors designed at the end of 1914 and proved so successful that they were fitted to new battleships from 1916.

The previous form of protection against torpedoes had been the torpedo-net, a cumbersome crinoline of steel wire which hung from booms slung out horizontally from the ship's side. They could only be used if the ship was at anchor or moving very slowly, and required so many men to handle them that they could only be fitted to large cruisers and battleships.

The British decided to stop using them in 1913 and got rid of them as fast as possible from existing ships, but German battleships did not lose their nets until late 1916. What finally discredited them was the

sinking of two British battleships at Gallipoli in May 1915. The *Majestic* and *Triumph* both had their nets out but the net cutters fitted to the torpedoes went through them as if they were tissue-paper.

On 13 October 1914, *U.17* stopped the small steamer *Glitra* off Stavanger, and after establishing that she was under British registry, sent her crew away in boats and sank her. It was the first use of submarines against commerce, and it showed that the U-boat could make a much bigger contribution than previously thought. Something needed to be done to relieve the pressure on Germany, for as her army had failed to deliver the decisive victory on land the British blockade daily became a greater threat to survival. The commerce-raiding cruisers were all sunk, immobilized or interned in neutral waters by the end of 1914, having sunk less than two per cent of the British mercantile marine.

There were still only 29 U-boats available at the end of 1914, but this did not stop the declaration of an 'unrestricted' campaign against shipping around the British Isles, unrestricted in the sense that neutral ships would be sunk at sight if sailing in the War Zone. It meant rapidly rising losses of shipping but it also put a great strain on the German Navy. U-Boats had to be fitted with deck-guns, torpedo-production had to be stepped up, radio communications had to be improved and officers and men had to be trained to identify merchant ships and their house flags. The building of more U-boats would take much longer, although certain stopgap measures could be taken right away.

(right) U-boats at their Flanders base. A complete dockyard with bomb-proof concrete shelters was established at Bruges between 1915 and 1918 to allow submarines to operate against Allied shipping in the Channel and Western Approaches.
Photo: Imperial War Museum

(left) *Acasta* Class destroyers in line ahead in the Solent in 1914. These sturdy 950-tonners were the basis for the highly successful Royal Navy destroyers built in large numbers from 1913 to 1918.
Photo: Author's Collection

A rare view of *UC.5*, a minelaying U-boat which ran aground off the Yorkshire coast in April 1916. She has been docked at Harwich to allow her minelaying arrangements to be examined, and a mine is about to be lifted out of the second vertical well. The two mines in each well were dropped through the keel and water ballast was automatically taken in to compensate for the weight.
Photo: NMM/Gunn Collection

A new class of very small U-boat was ordered at the end of 1914 to use existing engines. Known as UB-boats, they could be shipped in sections by rail from Bremen to Antwerp and some were even sent down to the Mediterranean for reassembly by the Austrians at Cattaro. They carried only two small torpedoes and were sometimes scarcely able to stem the tidal rips in the Channel but they could be built in less than six months. Even when the design was expanded into a more seaworthy and habitable UB II type it could be completed six months earlier than the 700–800-ton 'Mittel U' type. In all 100 U-boats were ordered in 1915 but only the UB-boats could be ready before November that year. Yet in that time British losses of shipping averaged some 48000 tons per month and the neutrals were losing a further 14000 tons.

Although the fundamental questions about the best method of reducing these losses were not being answered scientists tackled the problems of detecting and sinking submarines. The depth-charge proved a simple and cheap weapon, a drum of explosive detonated at a pre-set depth by a hydrostatic valve. It enabled a warship to attack a submarine after it had submerged, and had the advantage of subjecting the U-boat and its crew to severe stress even if it exploded outside lethal range. Scientists also produced the hydrophone, which could 'hear' the propeller-noise of a U-boat and give a surface ship warning of its presence and indicate a bearing. Both depth-charges and hydrophones were issued to destroyers and smaller escort vessels by the end of 1916, and a variety of explosive sweeps were also used against submerged U-boats.

Mine warfare also proved much more important than either side had dreamed. Within a few months the whole of the Channel and the North Sea was thickly sown with mines. They spread like a rash, reducing still further the freedom of ships to move at will, and needing a fleet of converted trawlers and naval minesweepers to get rid of them. And as fast as the minefields were cleared fresh ones were laid.

Submarines were also pressed into service for minelaying. The credit for designing the first submarine minelayer goes to the Russians, for they laid down the *Krab* in 1908, but by the time she was completed in 1915 the Germans had hurriedly built minelayers of their own. These UC-boats had six vertical wells inside the pressure hull, each containing two mines which could be dropped through hatches underneath. The mine and its sinker dropped clear, and the submarine automatically took in the equivalent weight of water as ballast to maintain itself at the correct depth. In 1916 the first British minelaying submarine also appeared, with 20 mines in similar wells in the ballast tanks on either side.

The British relied heavily on surface minelaying as well, using destroyers and light cruisers. It was found that a destroyer could carry as many as 60 mines by sacrificing a gun and a pair of torpedo-tubes. The mines were carried on rails on deck, winched aft and dropped over the stern.

Because of Lord Fisher's prejudice against mines the Royal Navy was forced to rely on two commercial types, and until 1916 much of this vast mine-laying effort was nullified because neither of them was reliable.

In 1916 a copy of the German Herz horn mine was produced, known as the H2, and as soon as this was available in numbers it began to inflict losses. In 1918 the British laid the first of a new type of magnetic 'ground' mine, laid in shallow waters to trap U-boats leaving and entering their bases on the Flanders coast. It was crude and unreliable but it pointed the way to future developments.

Compared to the submarine and the mine the aircraft had a short pedigree, but it also made a noticeable impact on the naval war. As early as 1911

Minelaying rails on board the British destroyer *Walker* allowed her to lay 60 mines. A special minelaying flotilla was created in 1917 to mine the Heligoland Bight and the Flanders coast as a counter to the U-Boats.
Photo: NMM Denny Collection

the American Eugene Ely had landed on a ship and taken off, and a year later similar trials took place in England. The first ship to take aircraft to sea was the old light cruiser HMS *Hermes* in 1913, with platforms forward and aft for carrying two seaplanes. Soon after the outbreak of war a number of Cross-Channel ships were converted to seaplane carriers to provide reconnaissance for the fleet, and the first bombing raid on Germany was mounted in December 1914. These ships were not aircraft carriers in the true sense, for they merely transported the flimsy seaplanes in canvas hangars, lifted them out onto the water and recovered them when they landed alongside.

Early in 1915 Commodore Tyrwhitt of the Harwich Force obtained permission to provide some of his *Arethusa* class light cruisers with a platform over the bows for launching a fighter aircraft, in the hope that they could shoot down Zeppelins. These big airships provided the German fleet with excellent reconnaissance, and on many occasions they were able to give timely warning of British fleet movements. Land aircraft were needed to deal with this nuisance as seaplanes were too slow and could not climb as high as the Zeppelins.

In 1917 it proved possible to fly a Sopwith Pup off a platform mounted over the forward gun of the cruiser *Yarmouth* and soon work was in hand on converting and building the first true aircraft carriers. The big cruiser *Furious* was finished as a carrier, a battleship building for Chile and a liner for Italy were taken over on the stocks and the world's first warship designed to operate aircraft was laid down. As an interim measure a large number of cruisers and battleships were given flying platforms to enable them to launch reconnaissance and fighter aircraft. The cruisers had a small platform forward of the bridge, but the battleships carried platforms on their gun turrets, so that it was merely necessary to train the turret into the wind to provide sufficient lift.

The only full-scale naval battle of the war was Jutland on 31 May, 1916, but it proved a disappointment to the British for the German High Seas Fleet inflicted heavier losses than it sustained (three battlecruisers and three armoured cruisers as against one battlecruiser and an old battleship) and escaped back to port. But in another sense it was very decisive for it was the first concrete evidence of what happened to the latest capital ships when they were damaged.

The destruction of the older British battlecruisers was to be expected for they were no better protected than armoured cruisers, but the loss of HMS *Queen Mary* and the near destruction of her sister *Lion* revealed disturbing facts about the cordite propellant of British heavy guns. Because of a fault in the manufacturing process it tended to burst into flame with a violent flash, which had little difficulty in defeating the supposedly flash-tight doors leading from the magazine to the hoist. Another fault which did not come to light until some months later was a weakness in the armour-piercing caps on the heavy shell, which meant that the hits scored on German capital ships during the battle had less chance of penetrating to a vital spot before exploding. Both sides found that pre-war ideas about underwater damage needed revision, but above all the effectiveness of long-range gunnery and of daylight torpedo attacks were shown to be greatly exaggerated. As at the Dogger Bank in 1915 the percentage of hits was low because the targets were at the extreme limit of visibility, and the gunfire of battleships and their escorting cruisers and destroyers was enough to break up the most determined attacks.

Jutland persuaded both sides that the decisive battle would not be achieved by capital ships alone, and they decided to explore other means. The British at last started to look at the problems of protecting and replacing their shipping, increased production of destroyers and escort vessels and looked at new ways of using aircraft at sea. The Germans could do little beyond building more U-boats and initiating a second unrestricted campaign against commerce. But the success of the 1915 campaign had been achieved by gunfire as much as torpedoes, and so a new type called the 'U-cruiser' appeared in 1917. These were big U-boats armed with 15-cm (5.9-inch) guns and capable of cruising much farther afield than before. All types of U-boat grew larger, until the new UB III type were as big as the pre-war 'Mittel U' types but the 'U-cruisers' proved a step in the wrong direction. They were clumsy and made more demands on scarce raw materials and equipment; when convoys were introduced in April 1917 the gun proved far less useful than it had in 1915–16.

Ultimately production problems defeated the German naval effort. All work on capital ships stopped in 1917 to free manpower and steel for U-boats and men were drafted from the battle fleet

to man the new boats. But production was too slow because it was in the hands of too few shipyards and because too many big boats were ordered at the expense of the smaller types. In contrast the Allies, once they realized how precious their merchant shipping was, mobilized their resources to build new standard ships and warships at remarkable speed. With their broader-based economies the United States and Great Britain could outbuild the Germans but they also showed a greater ruthlessness in choosing priorities.

The light battlecruiser HMS *Furious* undergoing conversion to an aircraft carrier in 1917, with a flying-off platform forward but her second 18-inch gun turret still in position aft. This conversion was only a partial success and in 1918 the 18-inch turret was replaced by a flying-on deck. This was less successful, and eventually she was completely rebuilt as a flush-decked carrier. Photo: MoD

Retrenchment

The Armistice did not halt the development of warships, for rivalry between Japan and the United States had started a new arms race. In 1916 the US Navy obtained permission for an ambitious programme of battleships larger than any yet built, with the inevitable cruisers, destroyers and submarines in support. This in turn provoked the Japanese to formulate their '8-8' Programme, to provide eight new battleships and eight battlecruisers for the fleet within ten years.

The British were dismayed to find that the Royal Navy was about to lose its commanding position as the largest in the world. True, it still had superiority in numbers, but the size and power of the new American and Japanese ships would outclass any of the existing British ships. In 1920 work started on designs to match the foreign competition, but first a series of detailed tests were carried out on surrendered German ships and comparable British ships. The British were in a unique position, for they had accumulated considerably more action experience than anyone else by using their ships more. They had also captured intact the *Baden*, the last German battleship to be completed, and had access to the German post-Jutland designs. Neither the Japanese nor the Americans had this information and in any case their designs had been finalized before the Battle of Jutland, and could not incorporate any of the lessons learned.

The result was a quartet of 48 000-ton battle-cruisers armed with 16-inch guns, to be followed by four 48 500-ton battleships armed with 18-inch guns. They were in many ways as big a leap forward in

design as the *Dreadnought* had been in 1906; they used a new form of inclined internal armour and adopted the 'all-or-nothing' principle, with armour concentrated only on the vitals of the ship. The method had first been tried in the USS *Nevada* in 1911 but now it was essential for it would be impossible to armour the whole length of a ship 850 feet long. An important departure was to move the armoured deck higher, where it could provide better protection against plunging fire and aircraft bombs, and also preserve a larger internal volume against damage.

The problem for the United States was that she had entered a race in which she was left behind before the start. Her entry into the war in 1917 meant that all work on battleships was stopped in favour of destroyer-building, and now that Germany had been defeated the taxpayer and the politician could not see the need for a huge programme of shipbuilding. To make matters worse the Japanese and the British had designed ships which outclassed the 1916 designs, and the US Navy was faced with the prospect of cancelling the existing hulls and asking Congress for permission to build even bigger ships.

After some hesitation President Harding took the only sensible way out and invited the major naval powers (Great Britain, Japan, Italy and France) to a conference in 1921, to discuss ways of limiting the size of navies. This was the famous Washington Conference which led to a treaty in 1922 after a bitter wrangle between the five delegations. The Americans and Japanese fought to save as many as they could of their incomplete ships, whereas the British fought for the right to build two new ships to match the latest foreign battleships. The Japanese wanted parity with the British and Americans, and although the French and Italians were in no position to challenge the other three they demanded similar rights.

The Washington Treaty finally ground out a compromise. Great Britain and the United States were to have parity in numbers of capital ships but Japan was limited to a 3:5 ratio. This 5:5:3 arrangement was denounced by the Japanese as a Rolls–Rolls–Ford settlement, but they ratified the treaty. France and Italy were each permitted half the Japanese total. The calibre of guns was limited to 16-inch and displacement to 35 000 tons. Cruisers were limited to 10 000 tons and 8-inch guns, but it was felt that only loose limits of size were necessary for destroyers, submarines and smaller vessels.

The British won permission to build their two battleships, and these emerged in 1927 as HMS *Nelson* and HMS *Rodney*, two of the most unorthodox battleships ever built. They were in effect truncated editions of the 48 000-ton battlecruisers designed in 1920–21, with speed sacrificed rather than protection. Because of their outlandish appear-

Seen in silhouette HMS *Rodney* emphasizes her unorthodox layout, with all three triple 16-inch gun turrets forward and the superstructure and funnel aft. This was to allow armour to be concentrated over the vitals, but the 48 000-ton design of which *Nelson* and *Rodney* were reduced editions was equally unorthodox in its layout. Photo: MoD

ance, with all three triple turrets forward and a squat funnel set well aft they were denounced as freaks, but they retained all the best features from the battle-cruisers and were as fast as the contemporary American *West Virginia* class. But above all the design incorporated the lessons of the recent war, and they had a novel form of underwater protection. Technically an internal bulge, but also known as 'water protection' or 'liquid-loaded layers', this allowed the ship to take on an additional 2000 tons of water in a vertical space between her side and the anti-torpedo bulkhead. In exactly the same way as the monitors' bulges in 1915 the combination of air- and water-filled voids would absorb and dissipate the force of a torpedo explosion. The British had not revealed this system at the conference table but insisted on the new definition of 'standard' displacement, by which 'reserve feed water' was excluded from the total to conceal the discrepancy.

It is interesting to note that the two principal features copied from German designs, a relatively light shell fired at a higher muzzle velocity than usual, and much greater metacentric height, proved the most unsatisfactory elements in the design. The 16-inch gun was never as successful as the 1912 model 15-inch, and the high metacentric height made for a very stiff ship with an uncomfortable slow roll. In other respects they were, however, the most effective battleships of their day.

Cruiser design was much more radically affected by the Washington Treaty. The Americans had set their hearts on building 10000-ton ships armed with 8-inch guns, despite the good showing made by light cruisers in the recent war. The reason for this was the assumption that the US Navy would be fighting in the Pacific, where gunpower and endurance were more important. Indeed it could be said that the Washington Treaty gave the British the battleships

(left) The limit of 10000 tons on cruisers imposed by the Washington Treaty caused many headaches for warship-designers as it was hard to build a balanced design on that displacement. The Italian *Condottieri* type achieved some measure of armouring only by keeping gun calibre down to 6-inch, as in the *Duca d'Aosta* and *Muzio Attendolo*.
Photo: Aldo Fraccaroli

(right) Apart from her poor endurance the French *Algérie* was one of the best 8-inch gunned Treaty cruisers, but her weight of guns and armour were achieved by allowing the displacement to rise unofficially to 11100 tons.
Photo: Musée de la Marine

that they wanted, and the Americans the cruisers that they wanted.

All five navies started to build cruisers to the new limits, with varying degrees of success. The French and Italians produced vessels with high speed but virtually no protection, the Japanese apparently produced a ship of light cruiser displacement (7100 tons) but with six 8-inch guns, the British produced a ship with eight guns, a speed of $32\frac{1}{2}$ knots but little armour, while the Americans seemed to do best with ten guns and $32\frac{1}{2}$ knots on 9100 tons. In practice the Japanese ships, the *Furutaka* class, worked out at 1000 tons more than announced, and needed major modification within ten years. The American *Pensacola* class were probably the best value for the money spent, but the British *Kent* class ran them a

close second, with exceptional seaworthiness, a high rate of fire and good underwater protection similar to that in the *Nelson* and *Rodney*.

Given the state of the art it was virtually impossible to build a cruiser with eight to ten guns, a speed of 32–33 knots and adequate armour as well, and all these heavy cruisers sacrificed one or other of these points. But the search for a solution was beneficial in spurring designers on to investigate new structural steels and lighter machinery. The *Nelson* and *Rodney* benefited from a new light structural steel and their boilers were considerably more economical on fuel than earlier models.

No more battleships were laid down until 1936, for the 1930 London Naval Treaty extended the 'holiday' for another five years. In their place cruisers

flourished, with steady improvements in protection as navies accepted the need for very high speed. The pace continued to be set by the Japanese, who could apparently build within the 10000-ton limit and still have ten 8-inch guns, 3–4-inch armour and a speed of 35 knots. The same gullibility extended to Italian cruisers, which were claimed to be capable of similar speeds, with ammunition and fuel aboard.

The heavy cruiser was expensive, and opinion gradually veered back to the neglected light cruiser, defined as a ship under 10000 tons with guns no bigger than 6.1-inch. The British, French and Italians were content to build ships of about 7000 tons to keep up the numbers. The British were looking for ways of getting size down further to increase the number of cruisers, for they had a massive merchant fleet to protect, but they found that 5000 tons was too small.

The 10000-ton limit led indirectly to one of the most ingenious feats of ship-design, and at the same time one of the most misunderstood. After her defeat Germany was bound by the Treaty of Versailles, which permitted nothing more than a coast defence force. This included six obsolete pre-dreadnought battleships and eight small cruisers of similar vintage, all of which could be replaced by new construction limited to 10000 tons and 6000 tons respectively. It was assumed that this would limit the Germans to building small coast defence battleships like those built in Sweden.

In 1929 work started on the first battleship replacement, a 10000-ton ship armed with six 11-inch guns and capable of 26 knots. What emerged was a powerful cruiser with two triple 11-inch turrets and eight 5.9-inch guns and the phenomenal endurance of 10000 miles. Named *Deutschland*, she was nicknamed a 'pocket battleship' by the world's press, for she could outrun any battleship and outgun any cruiser afloat. It was claimed that only seven ships in the world could deal with her, the three surviving British battlecruisers *Hood*, *Renown* and *Repulse* and the Japanese *Kongo* class.

The *Deutschland* had achieved this apparent miracle of shipbuilding by the extensive use of electric welding instead of riveting and particularly by the introduction of eight MAN diesel motors instead of the usual geared turbines. But she was not quite what she seemed. For one thing she exceeded

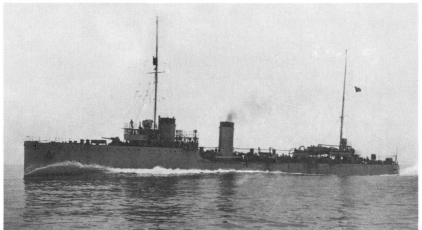

(left) The scout, or *esploratore*, *Carlo Mirabello*, completed in 1916, set a new standard for heavily armed destroyers. Although the original 6-inch gun was soon replaced the type was copied both by the Italian Navy and others.
Photo: Italian Navy

(right) The *Jaguar* was the prototype of the French large destroyer or *contre-torpilleur*. Although seen here on trials without guns or torpedo-tubes, she and her sisters made 34 knots in fully loaded condition. However, they paid a heavy penalty in reliability and had very low endurance.
Photo: Musée de la Marine

the displacement limit by 1700 tons and for another the designers could only provide light armour to the side and the main turrets. In other words she was a slow, over-gunned cruiser suited to commerce-raiding and not a ship of capital rank. Her construction was as much a political gesture of defiance against the Versailles Treaty as a logical answer to Germany's naval requirements, and although two more were built the last three were cancelled.

Although destroyers were not governed by the Washington Treaty they were developing the same elephantiasis which took the cruiser from 7000 tons to 12 000 tons in a decade. The Italians had started it back in 1914 by ordering three *esploratori*, or scouts, of about 1780 tons, armed with a single 6-inch gun forward, seven 4-inch guns aft and torpedo-tubes. The *Carlo Mirabello* and her sisters were nothing more than large destroyers and the 6-inch gun was more of a liability than anything else on such a light hull, and in any sort of seaway was almost impossible

to load. In 1916 the Germans went a step further and laid down destroyers of the *S.113* and *V.116* types, armed with four 15-cm guns on a displacement of 2000 tons. Only the two prototypes were completed, and they proved mechanically unreliable as well as unstable.

After the Armistice *S.113* was handed over to France as the *Amiral Sénès* while *V.116* became the Italian *Premuda*. Both navies seemed very pleased with them and soon ordered more of similar type. The Italian *Leone* class ordered in 1921 did not repeat the error of mounting too large a gun but their armament of eight 4.7-inch guns was double that of the contemporary British 'Modified W' class, currently regarded as the best destroyers in the world. The French *Jaguar* class were about 2100 tons, with five 5.1-inch, but the following *Guepard* class were given 5.5-inch guns and were a knot faster (36 knots). Known as *contre-torpilleurs* these ships soon reached 2400 tons in light condition. The high

point of *contre-torpilleur* development was the aptly named *Fantasque* class. On their trials they averaged 41 knots, a record for a class of ships never equalled since.

Naturally the Italians could not be left behind, and their 'Navigatori' class, named after the famous maritime explorers reached similar speeds. It was reasoned by both navies that fighting in the Mediterranean would require neither the seaworthiness nor the range needed for the Atlantic or the Pacific, and so all these 'super-destroyers' paid a heavy penalty in fuel consumption. When the Japanese and Americans also started to build their own versions such a luxury could not be permitted; much of the extra tonnage was absorbed by extra fuel to cope with the immense distances in the Pacific.

The only navy to stand aloof was the Royal Navy. With its eye firmly on budgetary limitations the Admiralty contented itself with building year after year slightly improved versions of a standard 1300–

1500-ton destroyer armed with four single 4.7-inch guns and eight torpedo-tubes. Performance was modest but seakeeping was good, with the result that a British destroyer's sea speed (the speed that could be maintained at full load in moderate sea conditions) was as good as any foreign destroyer. The British policy was also based on the need to replace a large number of obsolescent destroyers built during the First World War, and was the only way to obtain maximum numbers.

Submarine development did not follow the same lines as that of surface ships. The Washington Treaty permitted a displacement of 3000 tons and 8-inch guns, but only the French built up to this limit. The *Surcouf* was a remarkable submarine, designed as a long-range commerce-raider with twin 8-inch guns and a folding seaplane in a cylindrical hangar. She was even armed with a special type of small-diameter torpedo for short-range firing against merchant ships, and there was accommodation for 40 prisoners.

(left) The British submarine *M.2* recovers her Parnall Peto floatplane after it has landed alongside. Although pursued in many navies, this proved a blind alley. Photo: *Flight International*

(right) The American submarine *S.1* took the idea even further, with this tiny stowage for a floatplane. The drawback to such ingenuity was the time taken to assemble and dismantle the aircraft – in wartime no captain would want to linger on the surface for half an hour or more. Photo: US Navy

The British flirted briefly with the cruiser-submarine by building the giant *X.1*, 2400 tons and two twin 5.2-inch gun turrets, but her unreliable diesel engines proved such a nuisance that she was scrapped in 1936. During the First World War they had built two freak classes, the steam-driven K-class for operations with the battle fleet and the three M-class with 12-inch guns. The former had suffered a chapter of accidents, caused as much by their proximity to surface ships as the complexity of their design, and the latter had no known tactical role – they seem to have been built to prove that a big gun could be mounted in a submarine. The K-boats went to the scrapyard in the early 1920s but two of the M-class were converted to other uses. *M.2* was given a hangar and catapult for launching a small seaplane, while *M.3* became a large minelayer.

The purpose of the seaplane was to scout for targets, but the involved business of folding the wings and stowing it in a tiny hangar meant that the submarine had to linger on the surface. The Americans, Italians and Japanese all tried their hand at this idea as well, but only the Japanese pursued it. Both the Americans and the Japanese built sub-

marines based on the German 'U-Cruisers', examples of which had been taken over as prizes in 1919 but the vogue for so-called 'fleet submarines' soon passed. One important reason was that the speed of battle fleets had risen since 1914; then the fleet was accustomed to cruise at 17 knots, but by 1930 capital ships could maintain 20–21 knots with greater ease. Diesel propulsion could still not provide a significant margin over this, which meant that submarines were unlikely to be able to get into a favourable attacking position ahead of an enemy fleet.

Last of all there was the aircraft carrier. Although ambitious plans for carriers were in existence by 1918, with equally ambitious plans for using torpedo-dropping aircraft to attack the German Fleet in harbour, nothing dramatic was achieved until after the Armistice. The British commissioned HMS *Argus*, a converted Italian liner in the last month of the war and two years later she was joined by the ex-battleship HMS *Eagle*. Work on the first from-the-keel-up carrier, HMS *Hermes* was slow, and by the time she was completed in 1925 the Japanese had built the small *Hosho*.

The Washington Treaty provided a big stimulus to the development of carriers by providing big hulls suitable for conversion. The Americans and Japanese were permitted to convert the incomplete hulls of two large capital ships each, while the British had to be content with two smaller battlecruisers which had been completed in 1917. The French had already decided to follow the British example in converting the hull of an incomplete battleship and work had started in 1920. This gave the Americans and Japanese a flying start, for their big carriers showed the way to the fast carrier task forces of later years. The British could not match this because control of naval aviation had passed to the Royal Air Force, and even if they had been allowed to build large carriers it is doubtful if RAF policy would have permitted the development of adequate aircraft to operate from them.

Many minor technical developments improved the handling of aircraft on board carriers. Much was learned about the safe stowage of fuel, night landings and precautions against hangar fires. To allow carriers to carry more strike aircraft and fighters cruisers and battleships were given catapults for launching floatplanes. Unlike the turret-platforms of 1917–18 these permitted the launching of much heavier aircraft, intended solely for spotting and reconnaissance. The need to protect the aircraft from the effects of weather led in turn to the provision of hangars, another headache for the ship-designer.

Warship design made significant advances during the 1920s and early 1930s, although there was little external evidence for it. Machinery was becoming lighter and more reliable, fire control was better and designers were finding new ways of saving weight. Anything more radical would have to wait until the purse-strings were loosened. The Washington Treaty must take the credit for much of this; while acting as an effective deterrent to an arms race for a decade, it inspired a fresh approach to design.

Between the two World Wars the Japanese Navy reconstructed its old battleships to the limit. The *Yamashiro*, seen here in 1923, was one of six ships totally transformed, with new machinery, protection and secondary armament.
Photo: P.A.Vicary

The rise of Japan

Japan made a unique and startling contribution to warship design between the two World Wars. The reason for this was her lack of experience in design, following the drying-up of her sources of information after 1914. Hitherto she had depended largely on British assistance, but after August 1914 the Admiralty became more conscious of security, and by 1918 American diplomatic pressure made it unlikely that the Anglo-Japanese treaty would be renewed, so there was even less reason to keep the Japanese informed. Thus Japanese constructors were ill-informed about the Royal Navy's battle-experience and the post-war tests on German ships. To make matters worse they were now rivals of the United States in the Pacific, and had to start building a fleet to challenge the US Navy.

The result was an excess of originality rather than slavish copying. While the battleship 'holiday' was in force the main effort was concentrated on cruisers and destroyers, with a simple guiding principle: each class had to be superior to any existing rival. This was not easy to achieve, and many costly errors were made. As the Naval Staff would not permit any reduction of the armament the designed tonnage was often exceeded, but as far as the outside world was concerned the original figure was the only one quoted. Foreign observers tended to be taken in by these figures, especially as Japanese ships had many unorthodox features.

The heavy cruisers of the *Kinugasa* class, for example, started as a 7100-ton design but finished as 8300 tons. A worse case was that of the carrier *Ryujo*, which was designed at 8000 tons to avoid the Washington Treaty's lower limit of 10000 tons. An extra hangar deck was added during design, raising the displacement to 10600 tons, and when she was completed she was found to be dangerously top-heavy. Many modifications had to be made to improve her seaworthiness, and by the time she was ready for service an enormous amount of extra weight had been added.

The *Mogami* class cruisers had the unusually heavy armament of fifteen 6-inch guns in five triple turrets on 10000 tons, but on trials it was discovered that the hull was deformed and strained as a result of defective welding. Riveted strengthening was added, with bulges to correct stability, and after all this displacement went up to 11200 tons and speed dropped by two knots. Nevertheless, Japanese cruisers were formidable fighting ships; their heavy armament of torpedoes and provision for long-range scouting floatplanes were ideally suited for the Pacific.

The destroyers of the Special Type were a remarkable step forward. From 1923 a series of large destroyers was built with guns in twin enclosed gunhouses and three triple sets of 24-inch torpedo-tubes, and a speed of 38 knots. In the next group the 5-inch guns were made dual-purpose, with 70° elevation for use against aircraft, the first time this had been achieved in destroyers. In 1933 a new torpedo was issued, the oxygen-driven Type 93 or 'Long Lance'. Inspired by rumours (correct, as it transpired) that the Royal Navy was using liquid oxygen in its torpedoes the Japanese perfected a torpedo which could run for 40000 yards at 36 knots.

As contemporary Western torpedoes had a range of about 10 000 yards at 30 knots it can be seen that the Long Lance gave Japanese destroyers a tremendous tactical advantage. In fact, as Long Lance remained a secret until well into the Second World War it can be claimed to be the only genuine 'secret weapon' of modern times. When it was first used in action it was not even suspected of being a torpedo as no destroyer was in sight.

The high reputation of the Special Type destroyers was damaged when in 1935 a number of them suffered severe damage in a typhoon. Strengthening was necessary and top speed was reduced to 34 knots by the addition of nearly 300 tons of extra weight. Not until 1934, when all attempts to keep to international treaty conditions were abandoned could a realistic tonnage be stipulated, and thereafter the Special Type could develop without such problems. To take advantage of the Long Lance's capabilities reloading gear was provided on deck, so that a destroyer could retire behind a smokescreen to reload and then return to the attack.

The conversions of the carriers *Akagi* and *Kaga* were not as successful as those of the American *Lexington* and *Saratoga*, particularly as they stowed fewer aircraft. Although an island superstructure had been tried in the little experimental carrier *Hosho* in 1922 the Japanese preferred a flush deck with the smoke discharged through ducts at the side of the hangar. Other eccentricities were the provision of port-side islands in two carriers. On paper it makes no difference, but in practice pilots tend to veer to port more often than not, and the port side island caused 50 per cent more landing accidents.

The submarine *I.73* was one of a series of big cruiser-submarines built by the Japanese. Designed to emulate the exploits of the U-cruisers, they proved too big and unwieldy and many fell prey to American anti-submarine escorts. Photo: Imperial War Museum

As with the destroyers and cruisers, it was not until the international treaty limitations were discarded that carrier design could proceed without problems. The 17 000-ton *Hiryu* and *Soryu* were quite successful but the 26 000-ton *Shokaku* and *Zuïkaku* were much better ships. To provide for rapid reinforcement of the carrier force plans were made in 1934 to build three large submarine depot ships specially strengthened to allow conversion at a later date. These three became carriers in 1940–42, and served with considerable success in their new rôle.

Much thought was given to what sort of battleship would be built when the 'holiday' ended. As Japan

had no intention of renewing the treaties after 1936 her leaders reasoned that they could steal a march over the Americans and British by starting a class of vastly more powerful ships which would be ready shortly after the expiry of the treaty in 1940. Naturally they had to be bigger and better than any rival, but a further refinement was to make them so big that any ship built in reply would be too big to pass through the Panama Canal. It was naively assumed that this might persuade the United States to give up the competition, but it also took account of the fact that the biggest US shipyards were on the Atlantic coast.

The ships which resulted were the 64 000-ton *Yamato* and *Musashi*, the biggest and most powerful battleships ever built. To achieve an armament of nine 18-inch guns and belt armour nearly 16 inches thick a modest speed of 27 knots had to be accepted, but the faces of the turrets were nearly 25 inches thick and the decks totalled $7\frac{1}{2}$ inches. The very size

The destroyer *Shimakaze* marked the final development of the Special Type, with special machinery using steam at much higher pressures and temperatures than ever before. On her trials (seen here) she reached almost 40 knots and in service reached 40.9 knots with nearly 80 000 horsepower. Photo: Shizuo Fukui

and power of the 18-inch guns created new design problems, and the secondary guns had to be put in blast-proof mountings to protect them from the terrible muzzle-blast. The Japanese hoped to give them high-speed diesels but at the last moment a serious design-fault was discovered in the diesels and the ships were redesigned for conventional geared steam turbines. The two ships were built in great secrecy and were not ready until war had broken out. More of the class were planned but only one more was allowed to proceed as a carrier.

The Japanese strategy called for attrition of the American fleet by submarines, followed by a decisive main fleet engagement if the enemy should try to attack the home islands, and so a big fleet of submarines was built up. Their design was greatly influenced by the 'U-cruisers' of the First World War, with good endurance and a heavy armament of guns and torpedoes. But the detailed design was not particularly good; they were slow to dive and clumsy to handle. A number were equipped with small floatplanes for scouting purposes, and in 1942 the Japanese again went one better than everybody else by designing a 5000-ton boat capable of operating three floatplanes.

As early as 1934 work started on midget submarines intended to penetrate defended harbours. They proved sufficiently successful to be put into quantity production and two seaplane carriers were modified to carry them on board. During the war other types of midget were developed, culminating in the Kaiten one-man suicide midgets. A much more useful development started in 1937, the laying down of an experimental fast submarine, *No. 71*. She had a streamlined hull with no guns, and with powerful electric motors and big battery capacity achieved the remarkable speed of 21 knots underwater. In many ways she resembled the British R-class of 1918, and was the forerunner of the German Type XXI and later submarines.

Post-war interrogation of Japanese constructors by the Allies revealed a remarkably haphazard approach to the detailed design of warships. However, the empirical approach produced as many spectacular successes as failures, and the Japanese constructors repeatedly broke new ground. As with the Germans their industrial base was too small, and the ingenuity of their designs often complicated their already severe production problems.

The Type VII U-boat was a 750-ton development of the First World War UB III type, developed as a prototype for mass-production in wartime. Although rather small it enabled maximum numbers to be built out of the total of tonnage allowed under the Anglo-German naval agreement of 1936. The VIIB type, of which *U.52* was a unit, led to the VIIC, the standard workhorse U-boat of the Battle of the Atlantic.
Photo: Imperial War Museum

Arming for a new conflict

The expiry of the London Naval Treaty in 1936 allowed naval expansion to be resumed, although Japan, Italy and Germany had been pursuing their own schemes for some time. Both the British and the Americans were aware that they were being challenged and had drawn up plans for powerful new ships. The British in particular needed new battleships to replace their unmodernized ships left over from the First World War, for they had spent far less on modernization than other navies.

Five new 35 000-ton ships were laid down in 1936–37 for completion in 1940–41. Building times were expected to be slower than 20 years earlier because of the greater complexity of the ships but most of all because the once thriving British armaments industry had almost withered away during the long years of disarmament. Because of the haste it was decided to give the new ships a main armament of 14-inch guns, but in three quadruple turrets to increase the weight of fire. This was almost certainly a mistake, for the quadruple turret was complicated to design, and a subsequent decision to make one turret a twin caused even more delay. But the *King George V* class were a great advance over the *Nelson* and *Rodney* and foreign contemporaries. They were the first capital ships designed with a dual-purpose secondary armament and the first designed to operate aircraft. They had the heaviest protection of the new generation of battleships, with the exception of the Japanese giants. The steady improvements in boiler design over the last few years made it possible to drive them at 28 knots, which was judged to be sufficient.

The *King George V* class attracted much hostile criticism, mainly because of their 14-inch guns and modest speed but it is interesting to note that the United States opted for a similar ship in the *South Dakota*, which also steamed at 28 knots but achieved an armament of nine 16-inch guns at the expense of thinner armour. The German competitors of these ships, the *Bismarck* and *Tirpitz* have been credited with much greater offensive and defensive powers, but they needed $12\frac{1}{2}$ per cent more power for only one knot more speed and had thinner armour and inferior underwater protection. One of the reasons for this discrepancy was the German retention of the old secondary battery of low-angle guns, which had to be supplemented by a tertiary battery of heavy anti-aircraft guns.

The Americans and British had been disturbed by the Japanese *Mogami* class, and both navies had designed replies. The British built the *Southampton* class with four triple 6-inch guns and the Americans built the *Brooklyn* class with five triple 6-inch. To get the displacement down to 8000 tons (a new limit set by the London Naval Treaty of 1936) the British did a very clever job with the *Fiji* class. By adopting a shorter hull with a square-cut or transom stern and by using a more economical distribution of armour the designers were able to keep the armament of the *Southampton* class with only a slight decrease in speed. As such they emerged as one of the best designs of the day and one or two are still in service with minor navies.

To meet the threat of the big destroyer the Royal Navy reluctantly went to a larger destroyer, the famous 'Tribal' class. There was no attempt to match the *contre-torpilleurs* or the Japanese Special Type, but gunpower was doubled. This was achieved by halving the torpedo armament, but a much needed increase in anti-aircraft armament was also provided. The 'Tribals' were highly thought of in their day but technically they were far outclassed by the following design, the *Javelin* class. On 200 tons less they mounted six guns instead of eight but ten torpedo-tubes instead of four, with no loss of speed. Machinery was lighter, and the use of longitudinal framing instead of the traditional transverse method made for a much stronger hull. Serious damage amidships was likely to break a transversely framed destroyer in half, but Lord Louis Mountbatten's *Kelly* survived very severe torpedo damage in 1940 which would have sunk any previous destroyer. The *Javelin* design was so successful that it formed the basis of another 19 classes.

The Americans also flirted with big destroyers, building the *Porter* and *Somers* classes, but like the British they refused to match the extreme performance of the opposition, and contented themselves with doubling the armament. Prudently they reverted to a more modest fleet destroyer and evolved a standard type known as the *Fletcher* class, probably the best all-round destroyers to serve in the Second World War.

In the matter of aircraft carriers the British and American philosophy was quite different. The Americans had good, robust carrier aircraft and counted on their defending fighters as the main means of defending the carrier. The British had bad aircraft, thanks to divided control of the Fleet Air Arm, and were facing powerful land-based air forces, and so tried to protect the ship with armour. In fact they went so far as to put the aircraft into an armoured 'box' before an enemy attack, leaving the guns to defend the ship and the armoured flight deck to protect the aircraft from stray splinters. Had better aircraft been available a different and more aggressive

The new aircraft carrier HMS *Ark Royal* at Portsmouth in 1939. The 'horns' at the forward end of the flight deck house the pulleys for the catapults, but the leading edge of the deck in between is designed to provide a smooth airflow. The censor has mutilated the direction-finding beacon at the masthead.
Photo: Conway Picture Library

philosophy might have prevailed but it made sense in the conditions facing the Royal Navy in 1939.

The new carriers were known as the *Illustrious* class, 23 000-tonners capable of carrying 36 aircraft. On a similar tonnage and speed the American *Yorktown* class could embark 80 aircraft. In 1941 the *Illustrious* was to demonstrate graphically the value of her protection when German dive-bombers hit her with six heavy armour-piercing bombs in the Mediterranean. Although set on fire and badly damaged she managed to reach Malta under her own steam; the Luftwaffe had calculated that three hits from 500-kg bombs would sink her. Although not armoured in the same way American carriers also stood up to punishment remarkably well, as in the case of the *Yorktown* at the Battle of Midway, which was bombed and then torpedoed twice before sinking.

Submarine design showed no startling improvements, but the latest British boats adopted a heavy bow salvo of up to ten torpedo tubes to increase the chances of a hit from long range. The American

S.13 was one of a series of motor torpedo-boats built by the German Navy to evaluate new designs of high-speed diesel engines. These led to the formidable *schnellboote* of the Second World War, incorrectly known to the Allies as E-Boats. Photo: Drüppel

submarines stressed habitability and range for long patrols in the Pacific, and to achieve this they were about 50 per cent larger than the equivalent British T-class.

As the last navy in the field, the German *Kriegsmarine* had much leeway to make up. Two battlecruisers had been followed by the *Bismarck* and *Tirpitz* but Hitler's ambition outstripped the shipyards' capacity. Although grandiose plans were drawn up for a huge fleet they remained no more than a paper exercise, and many ships had to be cancelled in 1940. The cruisers suffered from machinery trouble and the destroyers in particular paid a heavy penalty for the adoption of very high steam pressures and temperatures.

The choice of U-boat for future mass-production took some time. The first designs were small coastal types, but ultimately an updated and expanded version of the successful UB III First World War design was chosen, and as the Type VII was to become the standard U-boat of the Second World War. Despite the restrictive clauses of the Versailles Treaty the German Navy had skilfully kept its U-boat design team together, using a 'front' organization in Holland to design submarines for other navies.

In one other respect the Germans had also shown foresight. Recognizing the value of motor torpedo-boats they had given development contracts for a high-speed diesel to two leading engineering firms. This resulted in the successful 20-cylinder Daimler-Benz V-form diesel, a unit which did sterling work during the war. The only other country to invest money in development was Italy, whose Isotta-Fraschini petrol engines had to be bought by the Royal Navy for lack of anything comparable.

Although the Royal Navy had left its rearmament until the last minute its strong card was still the superior building capacity of British shipyards.

A rare view of the hunter and the hunted. Away from the Western Approaches it was sometimes possible for a U-boat to rescue survivors but all too often merchantmen were sunk at sight. The spiral on the periscope is to reduce the 'feather' of spray when running at periscope depth. Photo: Bundesarchiv

Conditions in the Arctic or the North Atlantic in mid-winter were nearly as vile for the U-boats as they were for their victims. There was also the risk of vents freezing and the loss of stability from the added topweight of ice on the conning tower. Photo: Bundesarchiv

The war against commerce

The Royal Navy assumed that U-boats would be used indiscriminately against shipping, and had laid its plans accordingly. Its 200 fleet destroyers equipped with Asdic were to be supplemented by 100 commercial trawlers, also fitted with Asdic. The small number of sloops built were suitable for escorting convoys but were too complex to be built by the smaller shipyards unaccustomed to naval work. In 1939 plans were drawn up in collaboration with a firm specializing in whalecatchers, and the resulting modified whalecatcher was put into quantity production immediately after the outbreak of war. Better known as 'Flower' class corvettes, some 300 were built in the next three years, in Canadian as well as British shipyards.

Germany had only 57 U-boats ready for service in September 1939, and although they scored two spectacular successes, the sinking of the carrier *Courageous* and the battleship *Royal Oak*, there were too few to achieve a quick victory. The pre-war strategic plan had been rather vague, with the surface fleet intended to make the British convoy system unworkable, so as to give the U-boats the opportunity to destroy unescorted merchantmen. But in practice the individual surface raiders never managed to disrupt the convoys and by the time the U-boats perfected new tactics it was too late.

The surface raiders were dealt with by traditional means; the pocket battleship *Graf Spee* was trapped by three smaller cruisers, the *Bismarck* and *Scharnhorst* were sunk by gunfire and torpedoes and the disguised mercantile raiders were hunted down by individual cruisers on the distant trade-routes. But

the defeat of the U-boats needed the mobilization of not only the whole Allied shipbuilding effort but also the best scientific brains to provide new weapons and countermeasures.

Centrimetric wave-band radar had to be developed to allow escorts and aircraft to detect the periscope of a U-boat, new heavy, fast-sinking depth-charges had to be designed to reach to greater depths than before, and ships had to be designed specifically for North Atlantic convoy escort. The 'Flower' class corvette did sterling work, but as it had only been designed to work in coastal waters it was hard put to cope with severe weather conditions in mid-Atlantic. Under the pressure of air patrols and coastal escorts the U-boats moved steadily out into the Atlantic in search of targets, and when they operated in the so-called 'Black Gap' in mid-Atlantic they were out of reach of shore-based aircraft on both sides of the Atlantic, and here they scored their biggest successes.

The Royal Navy designed a new type of escort vessel, the 'River' class frigate, with long endurance and the right hull-length for seaworthiness in the North Atlantic. Orders were also placed in the United States for an escort vessel designed to US Navy specifications for the same task, known as the DE or destroyer escort. At the same time, of course, merchant ships had to be replaced faster than the U-boats could sink them, and this called for a massive effort by British, Canadian and American yards. But it was not enough merely to keep pace with sinkings, and victory could only be won by preventing losses and sinking U-boats, and this required the help of science.

The first centimetric radar for surface search went to sea in a corvette in May 1941, and a new ahead-throwing mortar called the Hedgehog was introduced to enable the Asdic to hold a U-boat in contact during the final stages of an attack. The Germans replied to radar with a radar receiver, which gave them warning of a ship or aircraft using its radar, and in January 1943 they started to use acoustic homing torpedoes against escorts. New explosives were used in depth-charges and ships were fitted with gear to speed up the loading of depth-charge throwers so as to increase the weight of an attack. In 1943 the first anti-submarine homing torpedo was used, an American weapon known affectionately as 'Fido' or 'Wandering Annie'. But in spite of all these counter-measures by the beginning of 1943 over 200 U-boats were available for operations in the Atlantic, with another 200 on training.

The crucial problem was the lack of air cover, particularly in mid-Atlantic. Late in 1941 the RN converted a merchantman into an 'escort aircraft carrier'. HMS *Audacity* had a flush wooden flight deck on which were parked six aircraft, and although she lasted only three months before being torpedoed

she proved such a success that more conversions were ordered. Known as escort carriers or CVEs to the Americans, the first came into service late in 1942, and by providing air cover all the way across the Atlantic they significantly reduced losses. As an interim measure oil tankers and grain ships were converted into MAC-ships or merchant aircraft carriers, with a flight deck over the hull and aircraft stowed above the cargo holds. The advantage of the MAC-ship was that it conserved valuable bulk-carrier hulls while contributing a vital element to the defence of convoys; they were civilian-manned with naval aircrews embarked.

The presence of aircraft meant that a U-boat could not trail the convoy, sending signals on its course and composition. This in turn made it much harder for the 'wolf pack' to gather for a co-ordinated attack at nightfall, the usual tactics. To reduce the risk of being attacked by radar-equipped aircraft at night the U-boats adopted the *schnorchel*, an air-mast which allowed the diesels to be used for charging batteries while running at periscope depth. The next step was to improve underwater performance, for the U-boat was much slower when submerged. The

To meet the drastic shortage of escorts the Royal Navy drew up plans for a modified whalecatcher design, called the 'Flower' Class corvette. Some 300 were built in England and Canada, and until proper escorts could be built they bore the brunt of the Battle of the Atlantic. HMCS *Levis* was torpedoed by a U-boat south of Greenland in September 1941, and although taken in tow foundered some hours later. Photo: Canadian Forces

Type XXI or 'Electro U-boat' had a streamlined hull with much greater battery capacity, giving her the phenomenal speed of 16 knots under water.

An even more advanced idea was the Walther closed-cycle turbine, which used hydrogen peroxide burned with oil fuel to run without oxygen from the outside atmosphere. There were great technical problems with this system; it was very costly, relatively large quantities of fuel were needed, and the form of hydrogen peroxide used was extremely dangerous. The speeds attained were very impressive, as much as 25 knots, but the production model, called Type XVII, was put into production before all the technical problems were eliminated. The effort

also diverted resources from the extremely potent Type XXI boats, with the result that only three of them were ready by the end of the war. It was similar to the situation in 1917, when confusion about the best type of U-boat to build prevented the Germans from defeating the Allies. The ideal figure of 300 operational U-boats was never reached, and in any case they were diverted to the Mediterranean and Norway, where they were much less effective. If the Type XXI boats had come into service in 1944 as hoped their superior performance would have outmatched the Allied escorts and possibly have turned the tables. As it was the U-boats suffered a crushing defeat, with 632 sunk in action out of the 1162 built.

War experience led to the building of the 'River' Class frigate, a big and effective long-range escort. It was so successful that it was built in Canada and the United States. The USS *Natchez* (PF-2) was built in Canada in 1942 and transferred to the US Navy on completion. Photo: US Navy

(left) The U-boats suffered the same massive defeat in 1945 as had occurred in 1918, but this time they were interned at Lisahally in Northern Ireland. Photo: NMM

(below) Battleship construction slowed down during the Second World War to conserve steel and labour, but between 1940 and 1944 the United States Navy completed four *Iowa* Class ships. Apart from the Japanese giants, these handsome 50 000-tonners were the most powerful battleships ever built, with a speed of 33 knots and nine 16-inch guns. With their enormous endurance and massive anti-aircraft armament they were ideal escorts for the fast carrier task forces.
Photo: US Navy

The carrier triumphs

Ironically it was the British with their relatively weak naval air arm who showed how potent naval air power could be. On the night of 11/12 November 1940 HMS *Illustrious* launched 21 Swordfish biplane torpedo-bombers and struck at the Italian fleet in Taranto harbour, sinking the battleships *Duilio* and *Conte di Cavour* and damaging the *Littorio*. For the loss of only two aircraft the strike put half the Italian battle fleet out of action, at a time when it could have exerted great influence.

The lessons of Taranto were studied closely by the Japanese, who had already decided that war with the United States was unavoidable. The target was to be the US Pacific Fleet in its base at Pearl Harbour in Hawaii, and this time the results were even more impressive. A total of 140 torpedo- and dive-bombers, with 43 escorting fighters, took off from six fast carriers north of Oahu at dawn on 7 December 1941. The attack lasted about half an hour and at the end of it five battleships had been hit by torpedoes. Then a second strike of 132 bombers and 35 fighters struck at 8.55 am, little more than an hour later, but this time relatively minor damage was inflicted and the defending aircraft and guns began to shoot down the attackers. But two battleships were total losses, two more had been sunk but could be repaired, and the rest were damaged.

By a miracle the fast aircraft carriers *Enterprise* and *Lexington* were away from Pearl Harbour on exercises during the attack. It could be said that the destruction of the battle fleet was a blessing in disguise for it forced the Americans to use their carriers as their main striking force rather than tying them to com-bined operations with the slow battleships. The destruction of the British capital ships *Prince of Wales* and *Repulse* off Malaya three days later by land-based torpedo-bombers confirmed the impression that the battleship had suddenly become redundant.

The Japanese carriers then went to the South Pacific to support the attack on the Dutch East Indies. Their air groups rampaged far and wide, even as far as Darwin in northern Australia. By April 1942 they were in the Indian Ocean threatening Ceylon but after a series of devastating raids on Colombo and Trincomalee the carriers withdrew to take part in an assault on New Guinea. This led to the Battle of the Coral Sea, an inconclusive action in which the Americans checkmated the Japanese aims but lost the big carrier *Lexington* in the first carrier-versus-carrier battle, fought at ranges far outside that of ships' guns.

Although the Coral Sea battle was a tactical defeat for the Americans it gave them valuable experience in time for the Battle of Midway the following month, when the Japanese Commander-in-Chief, Admiral Yamamoto, tried to trap the American carriers. The most urgent improvements were in the techniques of handling aircraft in the hangar and on the flight deck, and in using the defending fighters to best advantage. In the four-day battle which followed four Japanese carriers were sunk for the loss of the USS *Yorktown*. But whereas the *Yorktown* survived two fires and heavy torpedo damage over a period of many hours, during which she continued to operate aircraft, the Japanese carriers were gutted by fire.

Their standards of fire-protection and training of damage-control parties was not as good as the Americans'. The ships could be replaced but their highly trained aircrews could not. The Japanese training methods were very thorough but so lengthy that they were unable to provide adequate numbers of pilots in the next three years.

The fighting around Guadalcanal in the Solomon Islands was not decided by carriers, being mainly between cruisers and destroyers. The Japanese proved to be superbly trained and equipped for this sort of warfare, with their Long Lance torpedoes and night-fighting drill. Had the American ships not had radar they might well have been driven out of the Solomons, for in a number of engagements the Japanese under Admiral Tanaka showed themselves superior in tactics. In the Battle of Guadalcanal, when the battleships *Washington* and *South Dakota*

engaged the battleship *Kirishima* and a task force of cruisers and destroyers a minor electrical failure nearly resulted in the loss of the *South Dakota* for she had no lighting, no fire-control and no radar and blundered close to the Japanese battle line. She was saved by the *Washington*, which kept her searchlights switched off and fired only on radar.

The American shipbuilding effort rapidly went into top gear, partly aided by the fact that US Navy yards had been repairing damaged British warships and building yards had been turning out escorts under Lend-Lease. Huge orders for warships had been placed from 1940 onwards, and these ships began to pour from the yards in 1942–43. By mid-1943 it was possible to form new Task Forces from the new *Essex* class fast carriers, 27 000-ton ships capable of steaming at 33 knots and carrying 82 aircraft. These magnificent ships have only recently

The *Essex* was the prototype of a new class of American 33-knot carriers built for the Pacific. They proved an outstanding success, and after modernisation served for over 30 years. The side lift, seen level with the forward end of the island, helped to speed up the launch and recovery of aircraft. Photo: US National Archives

been scrapped after 35 years of service, and were in their day probably the most cost-effective warships ever built. They sustained the heaviest damage and although two were so badly damaged that they never put to sea again none was sunk.

To match the capabilities of the *Essex* class it was thought necessary to have battleships of the same speed. But to get 33 knots it was necessary to return to the battlecruiser concept, and the four 45 000-ton *Iowa* class laid down in 1940 and completed in 1943-44 had lighter armour than the 35 000-ton *South Dakota* class, with the same main armament. The bigger hull permitted much greater fuel stowage and a better anti-aircraft battery, added advantages for escorting carriers.

The battleship, despite its poor showing at the end of 1941 continued to play an important rôle in the Pacific. For one thing its heavy guns were invaluable

for shore bombardment in support of the numerous amphibious landings. With its stability and great beam a battleship was a far better platform for anti-aircraft guns than a cruiser or destroyer, and in 1944 at the Battle of the Philippine Sea battleships were formed into a Battle Line to put up a heavy AA barrage to protect the carriers from air attack. As a final irony the four sisters of the British *Prince of Wales* were shelling industrial targets near Tokyo in complete safety during the last weeks of the war. All that had changed was that carriers now provided local air superiority.

The weight of air attack in the Pacific was heavier than anything imagined, and both Japanese and American warships were continually given new AA weapons. The Japanese had settled on a 25-mm automatic gun pre-war, but this proved too light. The Americans had chosen an unreliable 1.1-inch (28-mm) automatic, but fortunately they learned from the British that the Swiss 20-mm Oerlikon and Swedish 40-mm Bofors guns were very effective, and both weapons were put into large-scale production in the United States. American ships generally carried a much larger number of AA guns than their British counterparts.

In October 1944 the Japanese turned in desperation to a new tactic, the *kamikaze*, or suicide attack. It was in effect the forerunner of the guided missile, with human guidance in the final dive, and provided the aircraft had been correctly aimed it would hit its target even if the pilot was killed. The carriers were the main objective of the *kamikazes* but all types of warship were attacked and special tactics had to be developed to counter the new threat. The 20-mm Oerlikon was found to be ineffective as it could not inflict sufficient damage fast enough to be certain of destroying the aircraft and even the 40-mm Bofors had difficulty in achieving the demolition needed. The long-term answer was to develop guided

missiles, and the American 'Bumblebee' programme started as an immediate result, but in the meantime work started on a new twin 3-inch automatic gun-mounting. Ships were instructed to use specific tactics against *kamikazes* to improve their AA defence; battleships and cruisers were to manoeuvre at high speed, but destroyers were to maintain course to give their less elaborate fire-control a better chance of registering hits.

The British armoured carriers finally proved their worth off Okinawa in 1945 when they were able to continue operating after *kamikaze* hits on their flight decks. Although one carrier, HMS *Formidable*, was hit twice she did not withdraw for repairs and was

Warships proved very adaptable in the Second World War. The fast minelayer HMS *Welshman* unloads stores and ammunition for the Malta garrison in 1941, ranging from food to glycol coolant for Spitfires. Photo: MoD

able to resume operations immediately. There was even discussion of the possibility of exchanging the six British carriers for six *Essex* class but nothing came of it.

The US Navy was the only one to win an all-out submarine offensive against shipping. Its submarines roamed the Pacific using a unique three-boat 'wolf pack', mining coastal waters, sinking merchant shipping and shadowing the main fleets. Again and again Japanese fleet movements were reported by US submarines and a number of major warships were sunk or damaged by them. For example, during the prelude to the Battle of Leyte Gulf Admiral Kurita's First Strike Force was sighted in the Palawan Passage by the submarines *Darter* and *Dace*. The two submarines followed the Japanese fleet all night, signalling its course, speed and numbers, and moved in to attack at dawn. The flagship *Atago* was hit by two salvoes and sank, while two torpedoes from the *Darter's* stern tubes hit her sister *Takao* and badly damaged her. Then the *Dace* put four 'fish' into the *Maya* and sank her as well.

When attacking convoys US submarines were able to destroy the escorts with impunity, before dealing with the merchant ships, a state of affairs never enjoyed by German U-boats in the Atlantic. Japanese carriers were top priority targets for American submarines, followed by oil tankers.

The depredations of submarines, minelaying aircraft and the fast carrier task forces wiped out the Japanese naval air arm. By mid-1944 there were not enough trained pilots to man the remaining aircraft and the reserves of fuel were dwindling. At Leyte Gulf the remaining carriers had no aircraft on board, and during the last ten months the remainder of the fleet was virtually annihilated.

The carrier reigned supreme after the war. Battleships retired from the scene rapidly, and where they remained on the active list they were used only for training. There was much talk of the atomic bomb and land-based air power making surface fleets obsolete but this was silenced when carriers showed their worth during the Korean War. Carrier strike aircraft proved more flexible in providing cover to the troops ashore, especially as land-based jet aircraft needed well-prepared runways. The 'brush-fire' war became the pattern of the years after Korea, and for such limited operations the carrier proved over and over that it could arrive first on the scene to provide both air defence and fire support.

The carrier also proved an ideal platform for the helicopter, either in the anti-submarine rôle or carrying assault troops. A number of older carriers were converted to operate helicopters and specialized ships have replaced them.

The USS *Barb* (SS.220) was typical of the big submarines developed by the US Navy for the Pacific. They proved deadly opponents for the Japanese escorts and inflicted crippling losses in merchant ships and warships. The *Barb* sank 90 000 tons of shipping as part of a wolf-pack of three boats. Photo: US Navy

It seemed for a while that jet aircraft would be too fast to land on carriers, but in the 1950s two inventions solved the worst problems. The angled deck permitted aircraft to take off again if they missed an arrester wire, and the mirror landing sight gave the pilot a simple and automatic reference for his final run. A third invention, the steam catapult, provided sufficient launching speed for the heaviest of the new generation of aircraft.

Today the carrier is coming under the same criticism as the battleship 40 years ago. She has become very expensive, far more expensive than the battleship ever was, and she is now claimed to be vulnerable to attack from submarines and long-range missiles. Her reign as the capital ship seems to have been even shorter.

Nuclear power at sea

The explosion of the first atomic bombs stimulated the exploitation of this enormous source of power, and it was the peculiar requirements of the submarine that produced the first controlled use of nuclear fission.

The first flurry of submarine activity after 1945 had been to digest the findings in Germany. The ideas of the Type XXI boats, streamlined hull, enlarged battery capacity and rapid reloading of torpedoes were all incorporated into new submarines by the world's navies, and in 1948 the US Navy initiated its GUPPY or Greater Underwater Propulsive Power programme to reconstruct most of its wartime submarines up to this new standard. Then the British and Americans started to tinker with their captured Walther hydrogen peroxide boats, trying to get them to work. The Royal Navy even went to the length of building two new hydrogen peroxide submarines in the mid-1950s called *Explorer* and *Excalibur*. Known as HMS *Exploder* and HMS *Excruciator* to their unfortunate crews, they provided invaluable experience as fast underwater targets but proved to be a blind alley for future development.

After equally unsatisfactory experience with their Walther boat the US Navy decided to explore the possibilities of building a submarine with a propulsion system which needed no oxygen at all. This could only be done by a nuclear reactor coupled to a heat exchanger providing steam to drive a steam turbine. The wheel had turned full circle, with steam-drive back in submarines after a lapse of 30 years, but this time high speed was not the main requirement.

Under the presiding genius of Captain (later Admiral) Hyman G. Rickover the US Navy and Westinghouse built a prototype reactor on land to test all the systems. The basic problem was the size of the reactor, which with its lead shielding required a much bigger hull than existing submarines, although she would still be smaller than the British *X.1* launched in 1923. The world's first atomic submarine was launched in January 1954 and named appropriately *Nautilus*, thus commemorating both a distinguished submarine of the Second World War and the heroine of Jules Verne's visionary novel *20,000 Leagues Under the Sea*. On 17 January the following year she flashed the historic signal 'Underway on nuclear power' and then proceeded to smash a whole series of long-standing records. In August 1958 she made the first submerged crossing of the North Pole, navigating by the new inertial navigation system (SINS) under the icecap.

The *Nautilus* has been refuelled four times with a new uranium core for her reactor; in the first two years she steamed 62562 miles, then 91234 on her second core and 150000 miles on her third core. Although a large and relatively clumsy boat, and not as fast as the Walther boats underwater she showed the immense tactical freedom conferred by nuclear power and convinced the US Navy of the need to develop the new technology.

Further experimental submarines followed, and in 1955 the first production class was started, the *Skate* class. Within a year another class was laid down, the *Skipjack* class, which differed in having a revolutionary 'tear-drop' shaped hull which proved much faster and more manoeuverable underwater than the conventional shape used for previous nuclear boats. The *Skipjack* design has influenced all subsequent nuclear submarines, and the first British nuclear boat HMS *Dreadnought* is virtually a copy.

The Soviet Navy could not ignore the startling achievements of the US Navy and in 1958 the first nuclear submarine, code-named *November* Type by NATO was sighted. Since then the numbers and types have proliferated, although only four countries, the United States, the Soviet Union, Great Britain and France have the technological capability to build nuclear submarines. The Netherlands planned to build them some years ago but could not afford the high initial cost.

These early nuclear submarines were built as 'hunter-killers' or hunters of other submarines, with large passive sonar or listening gear and an armament of homing torpedoes. But in 1956 the Soviet Navy produced a diesel-electric submarine capable of firing an intermediate-range ballistic missile on the surface. The United States was experimenting with a new scheme for launching ballistic missiles from underwater as an alternative to land-based intercontinental ballistic missiles (ICBMs); this acted as a spur to development of what became the Polaris weapon system.

As soon as the Polaris programme looked like being a success President Kennedy ordered five submarines to be built to fire the new missile. To bring it into service as fast as possible five *Skipjack* class were lengthened by nearly 130 feet to accommodate 16 vertical tubes and equipment, and all five boats were commissioned between 1959 and 1961. Their impact was extraordinary, for here seemed to be the ultimate weapon system; a nuclear missile fired from a submarine which could hide anywhere in the world's oceans. Of course it was not quite as easy as that, for the first A-1 Polaris had a range of only 1200 miles, which meant that it would have to

The most potent warship type and her most dangerous enemy. The nuclear submarine is now widely regarded as the most dangerous warship of all, with high underwater speed and an armament of long-range wire-guided torpedoes and underwater-launched missiles. The ship-launched helicopter, on the other hand, can track her with a dipping sonar and then attack with homing torpedoes. This RN Sea King helicopter from HMS *Ark Royal* is in fact rescuing an appendicitis victim from an American nuclear boat.
Photo: MoD

launch from certain areas to reach the most desirable targets, and she had to come to the surface to receive messages from time to time. But she had no need to approach another ship or make her presence known until such time as she needed to fire her missiles, each carrying more explosive power than all the TNT dropped in the Second World War. Polaris was seen as a 'second strike' weapon of deterrence, one which could not be knocked out by a pre-emptive strike and one which could therefore insure against such an attempt.

To keep Polaris submarines at sea for as long as possible a new system of manning was introduced, with two crews. Nuclear propulsion tends to need less interim maintenance, but the crews get very jaded after a three-month patrol entirely submerged and out of touch with the outside world. With 'Blue' and 'Gold' crews (Port and Starboard in the Royal Navy) it is possible to turn the submarine around with only a short period for checking electrical systems and rectifying small faults. The Polaris missile has now been superseded by the Poseidon missile and will in turn be superseded by the 4000-mile range Trident. This awesome weapon is about to go to sea in the 560-foot long *Ohio* class, at 16600 tons by far the largest submarines ever built.

Nuclear propulsion has proved very expensive. The only ships which have justified its use are warships for purely military reasons, and two Soviet icebreakers which need the power. There is no sign of any significant reduction in operating costs likely to bring nuclear propulsion into general use in merchant ships, and apart from the cost there is considerable political opposition in many countries to nuclear-powered ships. In fact nuclear ships have a far better safety record than, say, oil tankers, and the three known disasters affecting nuclear submarines (two American boats in the Atlantic and one Russian off Cornwall) have produced no known pollution of any kind.

Under the leadership of Admiral Rickover there has been an influential group in the United States wanting an 'all-nuclear' navy. They claim that the great tactical freedom of unlimited high speed and length of time between machinery overhauls make nuclear propulsion well worth the extra cost, and since 1958 four nuclear-powered aircraft carriers and nine cruisers have been built. For aircraft carriers particularly, nuclear propulsion provides additional advantages: there is no smoke interference with flying, and an ample reserve of steam for catapulting aircraft. But the cost of nuclear propulsion is truly colossal; it calls for more highly qualified engineers and above all, creates oversized ships. The gas turbine, with its totally opposite philosophy of short service life but rapid replacement has challenged the assumptions of the nuclear lobby. All that can be said with certainty is that the final argument over nuclear propulsion may be decided, not on a basis of cost but on conservation of energy.

(right) This stern view of the nuclear carrier USS *Nimitz* (CVN-68) shows the angled deck which permits landing while aircraft are taking off. Although the air group carried by such a ship gives her immense striking power, there is a strong body of opinion which feels that the size and cost have risen beyond the limits of prudence. Photo: C.&S.Taylor

The American nuclear-powered cruiser *California* (CGN-36) is one of the most powerful surface ships afloat, capable of providing area defence for a task force and maintaining high speed in all weathers. Photo: C.&S.Taylor

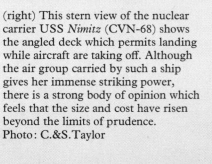

Has the warship a future?

For some years after the Second World War it was assumed in some quarters that air power had made ships redundant. Then the guided missile and radar-controlled gunfire showed that the argument was by no means one-sided. Then it was the turn of the carrier until it became evident that the carrier not only carried high-performance aircraft but also operated radars with a range measured in hundreds of miles.

In 1967 a new threat appeared. In that year an Israeli destroyer, the *Eilat*, was sunk by three surface-to-surface missiles fired from two Egyptian patrol boats. It was immediately assumed that this portended the end of the surface ship, despite the fact that the *Eilat* had been completed in 1944 and had no modern equipment of any sort. Since then there has been a great deal of activity, both in the development of missiles and in trying to find countermeasures. The most obvious result is an increase in the popularity of the missile-armed patrol boat as a successor to the wartime motor-torpedo-boat. Its supporters claim that it has taken over from the larger frigate or destroyer as the warship of the future.

Against this the major navies point out that small craft cannot hope to operate in mid-ocean. Even if their fire-control and radars were adequate the human element would fail for there is a limit to the amount of discomfort a man can endure continuously. And if a force of strike craft were to be maintained in sufficient numbers to be stationed around a long stretch of coastline, ready to dash out at high speed 'on demand', the cost of manning and maintenance would be prohibitive.

The other basic problem is that of shipping. There is no way of moving large quantities of raw materials, foodstuffs and manufactures around the world except by sea. To safeguard this traffic it is necessary to control the intervening sea, and this can only be done by forces which remain in the area. The most efficient blend is one of nuclear submarines, frigates, helicopters and long-range patrol aircraft, with the frigate providing an essential element of communications and command.

The helicopter has proved itself a most efficient killer of submarines, both as a weapon carrier and as

a hunter, using a dipping sonar. But the dispersion of
helicopters in 'penny packets' aboard frigates is
limited to the smaller helicopters. The best ship to
operate the bigger and more efficient helicopters such
as the Sea King is a big ship specially equipped with
workshops and hangars. This is why helicopter
carriers are vital for the job of 'sea control'. But
helicopters are of little use against large surface ships,
and only aircraft can provide the strike power needed
to sink them or force them to keep their distance.

This was the dilemma which faced the Royal Navy
when it lost its last fleet carrier, the *Ark Royal*.
Denied a replacement in 1966, its big carriers
Victorious, *Eagle* and *Ark Royal* succumbed to old
age. Yet even in the limited area of the North

The small carrier HMS *Hermes*
operates Sea King helicopters and the
first squadron of Sea Harrier v/STOL
aircraft. Photo: C.&S.Taylor

Although the hydrofoil warship is still in its infancy the USS *Pegasus* (PHM-1) has been running for three years and has proved highly successful. The Royal Navy has also ordered its first hydrofoil, HMS *Speedy*, for fishery protection in the North Sea. Photo: US Naval Institute

Atlantic and the north west corner of Europe the Royal Navy could not hope to provide cover for its own warships or protection for shipping without aircraft. The answer is the Sea Harrier Vertical/ Short Take-off and Landing (V/STOL) aircraft, a 'navalized' version of the well-known 'jump jet'. It cannot do all the jobs formerly carried out by the big supersonic Phantoms and the Buccaneer bombers operating from the *Ark Royal* but it can protect a task force from the surveillance of a hostile bomber providing data to a missile-firing ship over the horizon and it can strike at surface targets. Equally, a ship carrying Sea Harriers can carry sufficient anti-submarine helicopters to provide a good defence against submarines.

HMS *Invincible* is the first of a class of three new light carriers operating V/STOL aircraft, formerly called command or through-deck cruisers. They are also the largest vessels driven by gas turbines so far, with four Olympus driving two shafts. Another innovation is the 'ski-jump', a device so simple as to be almost ridiculous. It is a ramp at the forward end of the flight deck to give the Sea Harrier an upward trajectory on take-off, and by assisting the aircraft's transition from jet-lift to wing-lift it adds 1500 lbs to its payload. The ski-jump will take its place alongside the angled deck and the steam catapult as an invention which kept naval aviation in being by appearing at the crucial moment.

The frigate of the future may be equipped to fly off one or two V/STOL aircraft instead of helicopters. Current technological developments may provide a counter to the submarine or maybe not. The surface-to-surface missile could turn out to be much less effective than claimed. Nobody can prophesy with any certainty, but there is no sign yet of warships disappearing, for as long as shipping needs to cross the oceans of the world warships of some sort will be built to protect them.

The other advanced craft taking its first cautious steps in the naval field is the hovercraft. Its derivative, the fixed-skirt surface-effect craft has proved that it can launch a guided missile, and an experimental 2000-ton SES is under development.
Photo: Bell-Textron

Further reading

Aircraft Carriers N.Polmar (Macdonald & Jane's, 1969)
Aircraft Carrier A.Preston (Bison, 1979)
Allied Escorts of World War II P.Elliot (Macdonald & Jane's, 1978)
Battleships of World War I A.Preston (Arms & Armour Press, 1972)
British Battleships O.Parkes (Seeley Services, 1965)
British Battleships of World War Two A.Raven and J.Roberts (Arms & Armour Press, 1976)
British Destroyers E.March (Seeley Service, 1966)
Battleship Design and Development N.Friedman (Conway Maritime Press, 1979)
Big Gun Monitors I. Buxton (Trident Books/World Ship Society, 1979)
Carrier Fighters D. Brown (Macdonald & Jane's, 1975)
Carrier Operations of World War II D.Brown (Ian Allan, 1968 and 1974)
Destroyers A.Preston (Bison, 1978)
Destroyer Weapons of World War II P.Hodges and N.Friedman (Conway Maritime Press, 1979)
E-Boat B.Cooper (Macdonald & Jane's, 1968)
Encyclopaedia of the World's Warships H.Lyon and J.Moore (Salamander, 1978)

Endless Story 'Taffrail' (Hodder & Stoughton, 1931)
Ensign (series) various
Flush Decks and Four Pipes J.Alden (US Naval Institute, 1965)
Guide to the Soviet Navy S.Breyer and N.Polmar (US Naval Institute, 1978)
Imperial Japanese Navy A.Watts and B.Gordon (Macdonald & Jane's, 1971)
Man o' War (series) various
Modern Warships W.Hovgaard (reprinted Conway Maritime Press, 1971)
Ships' Data (series) various
Swept Channels 'Taffrail' (Hodder & Stoughton, c.1930)
Soviet Navy Today J.Moore (Macdonald & Jane's, 1975)
U-Boats A.Preston (Bison, 1978)
U-Boat Hunters A.Watts (Macdonald & Jane's, 1976)
U-Boats under the Swastika J.Showell (Ian Allan, 1973)
United States Battleships in World War II R.O.Dulin and W.H.Garzke (Macdonald & Jane's, 1976)
Warship (quarterly)
Warship International (quarterly)
Warship Profile (series) various
Warship Monographs (series) various

Index

THE SHIP

The first four titles in this major series of ten books on the development of the ship are: 2. *Long Ships and Round Ships: Warfare and Trade in the Mediterranean, 3000 BC-500 AD*, by John Morrison; 5. *Steam Tramps and Cargo Liners: 1850-1950*, by Robin Craig; 8. *Steam, Steel and Torpedoes: The Warship in the 19th Century*, by David Lyon; and 9. *Dreadnought to Nuclear Submarine*, by Antony Preston.

The remaining six books, which are to be published 1980-1981, will cover: 1. Ships in the ancient world outside the Mediterranean and in the medieval world in Europe (to the 15th century), by Sean McGrail; 3. The ship, from *c*.1550-*c*.1700 (including Mediterranean, Arab World, China, America); 4. The ship from *c*.1700-*c*.1820 (including Mediterranean, Arab World, China, America), both by Alan McGowan; 6. Merchant Steamships (passenger vessels), 1850-1970, by John Maber; 7. Merchant Sail of the 19th Century, by Basil Greenhill; and 10. The Revolution in Merchant Shipping, 1950-1980, by Ewan Corlett.

All titles in *The Ship* series are available from:

HER MAJESTY'S STATIONERY OFFICE
Government Bookshops
49 High Holborn, London WC1V 6HB
13a Castle Street, Edinburgh EH2 3AR
41 The Hayes, Cardiff CF1 1JW
Brazennose Street, Manchester M60 8AS
Southey House, Wine Street, Bristol BS1 2BQ
258 Broad Street, Birmingham B1 2HE
80 Chichester Street, Belfast BT1 4JY

Government publications are also available through booksellers

The full range of Museum publications is displayed and sold at
National Maritime Museum
Greenwich

Obtainable in the United States of America from Pendragon House Inc.
2595 East Bayshore Road
Palo Alto
California 94303

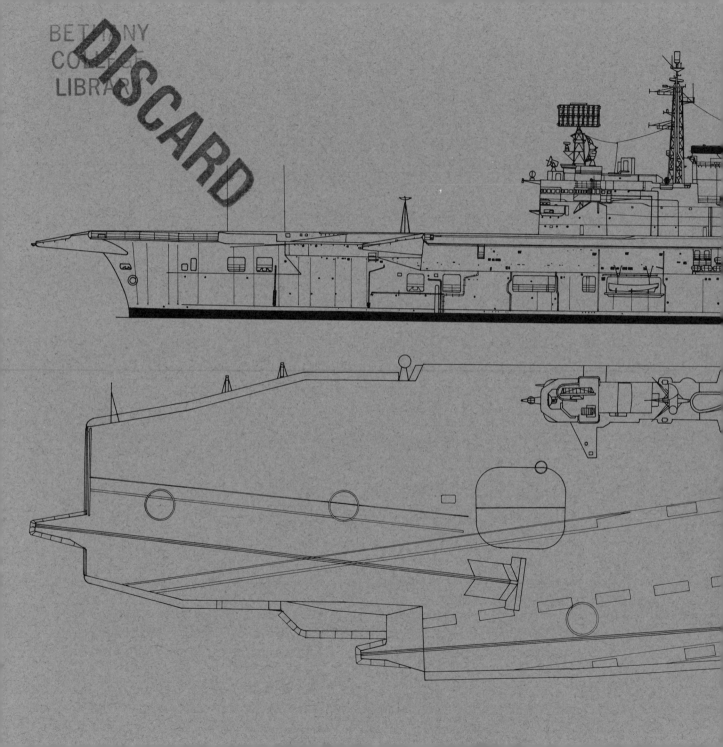